The Food Pharmacy

About the author

Jess Redden has a degree in psychology, and is a Pharmacy graduate and a qualified personal trainer. She works as a pharmacist in Dublin and is passionate about taking a holistic approach to health. She shares her recipes, fitness and wellbeing tips on her Instagram page, which has over 80,000 followers.

The Food Pharmacy

Easy, delicious, nutritious recipes to fuel good health

Jess Redden

Gill Books
Hume Avenue
Park West
Dublin 12
www.gillbooks.ie

Gill Books is an imprint of M.H. Gill and Co.
© Jess Redden 2023

9780717197408

Edited by Jane Rogers
Designed by www.grahamthew.com
Proofread by Kerri Ward
Indexed by Eileen O'Neill
Photography by Leo Byrne; © iStock/CarlaMc: 97;
© Pexels/Antoni Shkraba: 133
Illustrations by Lydia Moran
Food styling by Claire Wilkinson
Printed and bound by L.E.G.O. SpA, Italy
This book is typeset in 11pt FreightText.

This book is not intended as a substitute for the medical
advice of a physician. The reader should consult a doctor
or mental health professional if they feel it necessary.

The paper used in this book comes from the wood pulp of
sustainably managed forests.

A CIP catalogue record for this book is available from the
British Library.

5 4 3 2 1

I would like to dedicate this book to my parents, Brian and Linda. Mum, you have been an unwavering support and my rock for as long as I have known, and Dad, I know that even on my dark days there is nowhere that your light does not touch.

Thank you both for filling my life with such happiness and for always believing in me.

Contents

1   Introduction

Fitness

11   Post-workout chocolate coconut overnight oats
13   Balanced bagel
15   Goat's cheese and avocado smash
16   Baked sweet potato chilli
19   Quinoa veggie burger with roasted red pepper relish
20   Hummus-crusted chicken with zesty lemon quinoa
21   Creamy chicken stroganoff
23   Comforting sweet potato cottage pie
24   Spinach and ricotta fusilli
27   Five-minute no-bake protein bars
28   Chocolate protein pudding

Immune health

37   Caramelised banana porridge
39   Chicken noodle soup
40   Cheddar, onion and asparagus frittata
41   Halloumi and broccoli salad
42   Spicy stuffed peppers
45   Sizzling ginger sea bass
46   Lamb tagine
47   Red pepper and butternut pasta
49   Healthy honey fruit tart
51   Creamy tahini hummus

Cognitive health

61   Oaty breakfast bread
63   Butternut breakfast bowl
65   Salmon fishcakes
66   Tahini mango salad
69   One-pot chicken and leek traybake
71   Greek-style cod with bulgur wheat
72   Waldorf salad with prawns
73   Brain-boosting chocolate delights
75   Baba ghanoush

Hormonal health

87   Maca chia pudding
89   Seed cycling granola
91   Falafel salad with tahini dressing
93   Antioxidant-rich root vegetable soup
94   Fish pie
97   Turkey burgers with butternut boats
98   No-bake dark chocolate cashew bars

Gut health

107   Mexican scramble
109   Apple pie overnight oats
111   Oat bran raspberry muffins
113   Gut-loving chickpea and cauliflower salad
115   Lentil Bolognese
117   Coconut chickpea curry
118   Carrot and miso soup
119   Miso salmon and sweet potato
120   Greek yoghurt chocolate mousse

Heart health

131 Cherry tomato egg-white muffins
133 Almond butter and date oat pots
135 Tofu Buddha bowl with coconut peanut sauce
137 Spinach and pesto pasta
139 Fish tacos with tomato salsa
140 Tuna and sweetcorn baked potato
141 Fakeaway KFC burger
143 Hoisin duck noodles
145 Apple and blackberry oat crumble
147 Parmesan-free pesto

Bone health

153 Salmon and salsa pitta pockets
155 Roasted fig fruit bowl
157 Superfood smoothie bowl
159 Chicken bone broth
161 Lime and black bean prawns with brown rice
162 Mexican chicken salad
163 Tomato chicken pasta bake
165 Thai-style butternut tofu curry
167 Cherry Basque cheesecake with cherry coulis
168 Kale chips

Pregnancy and fertility

177 French toast
179 Strawberry and banana baked oats
180 Turkey flatbread
181 Sweet potato and cheese frittata
182 Nourishing veggie bowl
183 Cottage pie
185 Steamed yellow fish curry
187 Turkey moussaka
189 White and dark chocolate mousse
191 Anti-nausea smoothie

Skin health

197 Pesto avocado pasta
199 Almond chia crunch parfait
200 Salmon super greens omelette
202 Roasted balsamic beet and goat's cheese salad with creamy date dressing
205 Walnut-crusted salmon with sundried tomato couscous
206 Two-way mushroom risotto
209 Carrot cake
211 Glowing skin smoothie

Vegetarian and vegan health

217 Bean and kale ragu
219 Tofu scramble with roasted cherry tomatoes
221 Vegan pancakes with creamy cacao and hazelnut spread
222 Turmeric roasted cauliflower salad with honey, lemon and tahini dressing
225 Vegan beetroot casserole
227 Lentil, spinach and coconut dhal
229 Vegan lemon no-cheesecake
231 Sweet and salty caramel bars

232 Acknowledgements
234 References
236 Index

Introduction

Every time you eat or drink, you are either fueling or fighting disease: I heard this one day in a college lecture, and it's stuck with me for years. This saying is something I live by and try to instil in my customers when I am advising them in my work as a pharmacist.

When it comes to food, I have seen first-hand the transformative effects that changing your diet has on many common health conditions, such as irritable bowel syndrome (IBS), polycystic ovary syndrome (PCOS), diabetes and hypothalamic amenorrhea, which occurs when a woman loses her periods due to intense exercise, lack of calories or nutrients and stress. As well as impacting physical health, food plays a significant role in our mental health through the brain–gut connection, which I will detail later in this book. I hope this book will be a valuable resource that people of all ages can use to positively assist with improving both mental and physical health.

Life is all about balance and moderation, but what we eat has a huge impact on us physically and mentally. Before I began Pharmacy at the Royal College of Surgeons in Ireland, I completed a degree in psychology, which was a brilliant foundation for any career, as we grew to learn and understand human behaviour. When it comes to my work in the pharmacy and advising people who are struggling with health issues that could be improved by diet and lifestyle changes, rather than lecturing customers and bombarding them with scientific jargon, I first ask them whether they would like to improve their health. It's such a simple question but something we healthcare professionals often forget to ask. Behaviour change can only occur once a person is willing and able to make that change. We are all capable of making improvements to our health, and with the right support and knowledge, we can do so much more than we give ourselves credit for. Secondly, I encourage customers to figure out their 'why'. Perhaps it's because they want to improve their fitness or to be there to watch their children grow up. When I understand a person's 'why', I can counsel and support them and curate a plan for them.

It is never too late and you are never too old to build new healthy habits. Day to day, I counsel patients on a range of health-related topics from fatigue to hormone imbalances, and something I always emphasise is the importance of diet and lifestyle and the impact they have on our overall health. I remember a lovely young girl who was struggling with her skin came into the pharmacy one day. She was sick of trying topical products and asked for a supplement to banish her blemishes – but no such pill exists! I suggested she speak to a dietitian after discovering she lived on processed foods and seemed to be reacting to certain food groups. She came back weeks later, glowing and smiling from ear to ear. She had totally transformed her diet, and from just looking at her I could see the effects. Not only had her skin improved but she had more energy, was sleeping better and felt more positive overall. I feel so grateful to work in a job that I love so much, and which allows me to make just one positive impact every day on someone's mental or physical well-being.

When trying to make changes to our health and lifestyle, it's important not to be too hard on ourselves and to remember that progress is not linear. We all have setbacks, and we wouldn't be human if we didn't. This often gets forgotten, especially with the advent of social media, where people often share only their triumphs and successes. I believe we get our strength from encouraging ourselves and overcoming setbacks and failures.

I have experienced first-hand the positive and negative impacts our diet can have on our well-being. Creating recipes and dishes is my way of decompressing and relaxing, but life sometimes gets busy. For a period of time, I wasn't fueling my body with what it needed, which resulted in both physical and mental health challenges. We all go through rough patches, and I feel fortunate to have people around me to pull me through. Once I started to fall back in love with creating nutritious home-cooked meals, my energy improved, my mood lifted and I felt like myself again.

I have devised this book for anyone interested in understanding the role nutrition plays in our health and in making changes that will support long-term health and well-being as we journey through life. Based on my experience working as a pharmacist, I have created ten chapters that deal with the most common health ailments which can be improved with

nutrition, providing the science and the recipes for you to understand and better your situation as needed. The book is packed with simple and delicious recipes that will support bone health, immunity, heart health, gut health, hormone- and blood-sugar balance and much more! For example, our immune system is something we often neglect to look after until we are unwell; deficiencies in key nutrients, such as vitamins A, B, C and E and zinc, iron and selenium, can weaken parts of the immune system. By eating a balanced and varied diet, we can look after so many aspects of our health.

My passion and love for cooking and baking stems from my childhood admiration of my mum. She taught me how to cook and bake along with my gran, who was another fabulous baker. Every night of the week we ate home-cooked meals, and every weekend we enjoyed the aroma of Mum's Sunday roasts. I used to love having sleepovers in our house because Mum would go all out on the treats, from baked Alaska to simple chocolate-chip cookies, and in the morning she would have homemade breakfast rolls for my friends and me. I was so proud when my friends talked about how lucky I was to have a mum who could do all of that, and there and then I knew that one day I wanted to have a child who felt as proud of me as I am of Mum. Everyone in my family is a massive foodie – we would be eating dinner and discussing what we would have the following night or what was coming for dessert. No one appreciated a good meal more than my dad. He was always in awe of my mum and all her wonderful skills.

Life really is so very short, and health is our greatest gift. The philosopher Hippocrates once wrote that 'our food should be our medicine and our medicine should be our food'. We can help prevent disease through nutrition – what a powerful tool to possess! This book has found its way to you for a reason, and I hope you have the opportunity to learn, grow and develop new habits and skills to improve your health and well-being, and I also really hope you just enjoy cooking and sampling some delicious new recipes that you can add to your repertoire!

A note on the recipe icons
Each chapter in this book contains recipes suited to that particular area, but many of the recipes will optimise your health in several of the areas we explore. I've included icons that indicate where a recipe will contribute to more than one area.

Fitness

Between finishing my psychology degree and beginning my pharmacy degree, I undertook a personal training course. Fitness is something I have been hugely passionate about for as long as I can remember, and I wanted to learn more about how to perform and structure exercise plans. What I didn't expect was to come away from the course with a greater understanding of nutrition and of the role diet plays in reaching goals and supporting recovery. A well-known saying in the fitness industry is 'You can't out-exercise a bad diet,' which highlights the importance of nutrition when it comes to overall health and fitness. While both diet and exercise are important for maintaining a healthy lifestyle, many experts agree that diet plays a more critical role in weight loss and overall health.

Research has shown that weight loss is primarily driven by changes in diet, with exercise playing a smaller role. For example, one study found that participants who followed a diet-only weight loss programme lost more weight than those who followed an exercise-only weight loss programme or a combination of diet and exercise.

In addition, diet has a greater impact on overall health than exercise. Eating a balanced and nutritious diet can reduce the risk of chronic diseases such as heart disease, diabetes and cancer. On the other hand, even if someone exercises regularly, if they consume a diet high in processed foods and sugar, they may still be at risk of developing these diseases.

That's not to say that exercise isn't important – it has numerous benefits for physical and mental health, including improving cardiovascular health, increasing muscle mass and strength and reducing stress and anxiety. However, when it comes to weight loss and overall health, diet is often considered more important.

Macronutrients are nutrients we need in larger quantities that provide us with energy. They include protein, carbohydrates and fats. **Micronutrients** are required in much smaller amounts but are just as important for the body. They are mostly vitamins and minerals. Each macronutrient is involved in your body's post-workout recovery process, and it is important to have the right balance. I think it has been encouraging to see people moving away from diet culture because the hard truth is that diets don't work. They may work for weight loss in the short term, but they are not sustainable, and your body really is a temple. Life is far too short to deprive it of the fuel it needs. That fuel includes the three macronutrient groups – protein, carbohydrates and fats. When trying to lose weight or build muscle, we don't want to cut out these groups but rather focus on getting the right proportion to best suit our needs. In this chapter I explain the importance of each group and highlight how best to consume them in our everyday life. During low-intensity activities such as watching TV, reading a book or sleeping, our body mainly uses fat as its fuel source. This switches to carbohydrates during high-intensity activities such as jogging, cycling or swimming.

I want to empower you to make healthy nutrition choices without having to sacrifice life's simple pleasures! It's all about following a plan that works for you, one that is easy to follow and that you can sustain. As with each chapter the portion sizes in this section are simply a guide. If you have trained hard and are working at a fast pace, you might need larger portions than someone who has been sitting on the couch all day.

Protein

The role of protein after exercise – repair and build
Exercising triggers the breakdown of muscle protein. The rate and extent of this breakdown depends on the level of effort and the type of exercise you are performing.

Your body needs amino acids to repair and rebuild the proteins that have been broken down. It also provides the building blocks to build new muscle tissue. You should aim to spread your protein intake throughout the day. Individual factors will influence the amount of protein your body needs, but on average we should aim to consume at least 20-40g of protein at each meal. The recommended daily amount of protein for the average adult in Ireland is set at 0.75g per kg of body weight. However, our requirements will change based on activity levels, pregnancy and breastfeeding, age and overall health status. If you are someone who regularly engages in physical activity, this ratio should be 1.2–1.7g per kg of body weight. If you don't consume enough protein after exercise or throughout the day, it doesn't matter how long you hold a plank for, your body will take protein from muscle if it is not getting enough from your diet. If you are looking to build muscle, consuming protein within the first two hours after a workout may stimulate your body to create the building blocks required for new muscle tissue.

Protein has a higher thermic effect than carbohydrates or fats, which means that our bodies use more energy to digest and metabolise protein. This means we burn more calories during the digestion of protein.

Of all the macronutrients, protein is the most filling and helps to make you feel fuller for longer. This is because it reduces the level of the hunger hormone ghrelin as well as boosting the hormone peptide YY which makes you feel full. Protein provides 4kcal per gram.

Other roles of protein
- **Production of hormones**
- **Assisting the immune system**
- **Metabolism regulation**
- **Forming the structure for hair, skin and nails**

Protein is made up of amino acids. There are around 22 amino acids in total, but the body makes 13 of them. That means that there are nine 'essential' amino acids that we must get from our diet. Foods that contain all nine essential amino acids are known as 'complete proteins' and mainly come from animal sources, including poultry, meat, eggs and dairy. Plant-based complete protein sources include quinoa, hemp, chia seeds and buckwheat. If you follow a plant-based diet you can consume all nine essential amino acids by combining different sources, for example peanut butter and wholewheat bread or black beans and brown rice. Individually, these foods are considered incomplete protein sources but by combining them we can obtain all the essential amino acids the body needs.

Essential amino acids:

- **Histidine**
- **Isoleucine**
- **Leucine**
- **Lysine**
- **Methionine**
- **Phenylalanine**
- **Threonine**
- **Tryptophan**
- **Valine**

What about protein powder?

I always say that supplements should be used alongside a healthy diet and never in place of real food. That being said, I have used whey protein for years; I add one scoop into my morning oats or have it in a post-workout smoothie, as well as aiming to hit my daily protein needs. Whey protein is a good option post-workout as it reaches the muscles quickly so the amino acids can get to work on repairing and rebuilding muscle fibres straightaway. Whey is derived from dairy, so if you are looking for a vegan alternative, I would recommend pea or hemp protein. Casein protein is another type of supplement people may consider taking. This is a slow-digesting protein that releases amino acids more slowly, so people often take it in the evening to support muscle recovery. Like whey protein, casein is derived from dairy. It contains high amounts of the amino acid leucine, which initiates muscle protein synthesis, so it is a popular supplement among those looking to build muscle.

Carbohydrates

Our body uses glycogen as its fuel during a workout, and that is why it is important to include carbohydrates post-workout to replenish them. The rate at which our glycogen stores are used depends on the type of activity we are doing. Endurance sports such as cycling, running, swimming or boxing cause your body to use more glycogen than resistance training such as weightlifting. A rough guide is to consume 8–12g of carbohydrate per kg of body weight each day to help maximise your glycogen stores.

For post-workout meals some studies have found benefits in eating carbohydrates to protein in a 3:1 ratio, for example if you eat 90g of carbohydrates, ideally the meal should contain around 30g of protein. But this is a loose guide to keep in mind, rather than a rule.

Other roles of carbohydrates:
- **Required for the proper functioning of the nervous system, kidneys and muscles**
- **Contain fibre, which is important for gut health and digestion**
- **Help control blood glucose and energy metabolism**

SIMPLE CARBOHYDRATES	COMPLEX CARBOHYDRATES
Made of single or double sugar molecules	Made of longer-chain sugar molecules
Fruit, dairy and processed foods (cakes, fizzy drinks, sweets)	Legumes, whole grains, starchy and non-starchy vegetables
Quickly digested and absorbed into the bloodstream, giving a fast supply of energy	Take longer for the body to break down, therefore supply energy over a longer period of time
Tend to be lower in fibre and nutrients, especially if processed	Often nutrient-dense, containing more fibre, B vitamins, iron and antioxidants

How our body uses carbs

There are two types of carbohydrates: simple and complex. The difference lies in the number of sugar molecules they contain.

When we consume simple carbohydrates (glucose, fructose, galactose, maltose, lactose or sucrose) we get a spike in energy and insulin is pumped out by the body to bring the blood sugar down. So you quickly go from experiencing a high level of blood sugar, making you feel hyper and giddy, to suddenly feeling irritable, tired and maybe even moody. Simple sugars are found not only in processed foods but also in fruit and dairy. Sources of natural sugars are healthier than processed versions, but we still have to be mindful of portion sizes. When it comes to carbohydrate consumption, we should be aware of the differences between the two types and the importance of incorporating wholegrain sources of the carbohydrates that our body loves after exercise.

Fats

Fat is the main fuel our body uses during light activities and has many important roles in the body like:

- **Facilitating absorption of fat-soluble vitamins (A, D, E, K)**
- **Hormone production**
- **Organ protection**
- **Source of energy**
- **Essential for healthy nerves**
- **Healthy skin and hair**
- **Regulation of body temperature**
- **Production of new healthy cells**

Through the years fats have been given a bad rep and, in relation to working out and exercise,

you'll see misinformation about cutting out fats entirely in order to lose weight. Our body needs certain fats. We should never cut out entire food groups but rather understand how best to consume these food groups in order to maximise our health and well-being.

Not all fats are the same. While it is a good idea to cut down on or eliminate trans fats from the diet, other fats are essential for the body, for example omega-3 fats found in oily fish, which can help to reduce inflammation. The American Heart Association recommends that the average person should aim to consume no more than 25–35 per cent of their total daily calories from fat. This means that for a person consuming 2000 calories per day, their daily fat intake should range from 55g to 77g. It is important to note that the amount of fat a person should consume can vary based on their individual health goals and needs. For example, athletes or individuals trying to build muscle may need to consume more fat to support their energy and nutrient needs.

Let's take a look at the different types of fat.

Unsaturated or 'good' fats

These fats help to maintain healthy cholesterol levels. (Cholesterol is a type of fatty substance found in the blood.) The two categories of unsaturated fats are monounsaturated and polyunsaturated fats; 'mono' and 'poly' refer to the number of unsaturated chemical bonds.

Monounsaturated fats are found in olive oil, nuts, seeds and avocados. Their role is to reduce the amount of low-density lipoprotein (LDL) cholesterol, which is harmful.

Polyunsaturated fats (PUFAs) are present in oily fish, flaxseed, chia seeds and vegetable oils. The two main PUFAs are omega-3 and omega-6 (more on these in the heart health chapter).

Saturated or 'bad' fats

These types of fat are often solid at room temperature. Foods like coconut oil, ice cream, butter, cheese and red meat can contain high amounts of saturated fat. Numerous studies have showed that a high intake of saturated fat increases LDL cholesterol levels and can contribute to heart disease and stroke.

Hydration

Never underestimate the importance of hydration – it is essential to every bodily process. When we exercise, we can lose a large amount of water through sweat, so it's even more important to hydrate before, during and after a workout. As a general rule I aim to drink 2–3 litres of water per day. Water regulates our body temperature, lubricates our joints and removes waste from the body. If you want to set one health goal this week, I would strongly encourage you to increase your water intake and you will quickly notice the benefits of staying well hydrated. If you struggle to drink plain water, try infusing it with lemon, lime, strawberry or fresh mint for some flavour.

Tips when starting a workout routine

First and foremost, nobody on this planet feels motivated to exercise every day. I think a negative side effect of social media is that people want to portray a polished and filtered version of their lives in which they wake up at six o'clock every morning, go for a run, do a weights class and then somehow have the time to do a Pilates session in the evening! Never compare your life to someone else's filtered version. Instead, focus on your own lane and create your own goals. I promise that is where your happiness lies.

It's also never too late to start a fitness routine. My mum is one of my biggest fitness inspirations and she is in her 60s. No matter what your age, commitment, dedication and effort are what matter most when it comes to building a new fitness plan. Maybe you're a complete newbie and have never been to a gym before, or maybe you've just had a baby. Whatever your motivation for returning to or starting exercising, here are some tips for getting started.

1. **Set realistic goals:** For example, if you are new to running you could set a goal of hitting a certain distance over a certain period of time. When I go back to running after taking time off, I give myself five weeks to reach 5km.
2. **Schedule your time:** If my goal is 5km in five weeks I would aim to fit in two runs, light jogs or brisk walks a week and gradually increase the duration each time.
3. **Recruit a buddy:** It keeps us accountable. I have never cancelled a class that I have booked with my mum!
4. **Try different classes:** There are so many options on offer, from yoga, Pilates and boxing to spin, Zumba and Bodypump. Trying out new classes is a great way to meet new people and fuel motivation.
5. **Track your progress:** A few years ago I set myself a goal of completing three pull-ups. I worked on isolating different muscle groups and sure enough over time I reached my goal. At times I would feel frustrated that I wasn't making progress but looking back on how far I had come always made me feel proud.
6. **Set your clothes out the night before:** Preparation is key! The easier and less work we make a habit the more likely we are to engage with that behaviour.

It is never too late and you are never too old to start exercising. My mum recently joined me for a 'blaze' class, which involves treadmill running, strength stations and power boxing and it is a tough class. I often glance over at her during the class with so much admiration; she is my inspiration every day, and on days when I don't feel very motivated, I think about my mum doing a squat jump and punching the bag. It works every time! So find your 'why' and making exercise a priority won't seem as difficult as it once was.

Regular physical activity is one of the best things you can do for your health. Being physically active can improve your brain health, immune function, help manage your weight, reduce the risk of disease and strengthen bones and muscles. It also releases happy hormones to help boost your mood. No matter what your age, weight, ethnicity or gender, everybody gains health benefits from regular exercise. When you combine exercise with a balanced, healthy diet you are controlling blood sugars, supporting immune and heart health, reducing inflammation and paving the way for a long and healthy life.

Post-workout chocolate coconut overnight oats

| Fitness | Bone health | Cognitive health | Heart health | Gut health | Vegetarian |

Serves 1

Prep: 5 minutes plus overnight soaking

Nutrients per serving

Calories (kcal) **500**

Carbohydrates (g) **50**

Protein (g) **42**

Fat (g) **19**

Ingredients

½ banana, sliced
70g Greek yoghurt
1 scoop (30g) peanut butter
   chocolate whey protein
250ml coconut milk
50g rolled oats
1 tbsp peanut butter
handful each of blueberries,
   raspberries and shredded
   coconut

I love to make a few batches of overnight oats on a Sunday evening and vary the toppings each morning. This is one of my staple recipes that is quick and easy to make and ready to be enjoyed on the go post-workout. I use the chocolate peanut butter whey for optimum nutrition as my morning protein supplement.

1 In a large bowl mix together the banana, yoghurt, whey protein and coconut milk. Add the oats and stir well until combined.
2 Top with the peanut butter, fruit and coconut and store in a sealed jar in the fridge overnight.

Balanced bagel

Fitness

Bone health

Heart health

Serves 1

Prep: 5 minutes

Nutrients per serving

Calories (kcal) **560**

Carbohydrates (g) **60**

Protein (g) **37**

Fat (g) **26**

Ingredients

1 egg
1 wholegrain bagel
2 tbsp low-fat cream cheese
2 tsp relish, e.g. Ballymaloe relish
½ avocado, sliced
85g cooked turkey breast, sliced

After you have trained you need to replenish your muscles with protein and carbohydrates, and this delicious bagel ticks both boxes. Aim to eat it 1–3 hours after training to replace any glycogen you may have lost working out. The protein – from the turkey, cream cheese and egg – will help to build and repair muscle.

1   Fill a small saucepan with water and bring to the boil. Carefully crack the egg into the water and reduce the heat. Cook for about 4 minutes if you like your yolk runny, then carefully lift it out with a slotted spoon and set aside.
2   Slice your bagel in half and toast it.
3   Build your bagel by spreading each half with the cream cheese mixed with relish. Then add the sliced avocado and sliced turkey and finally add the poached egg on top.

Goat's cheese and avocado smash

Fitness

Gut health

Vegetarian

Serves 2

Prep: 10 minutes

Nutrients per serving

Calories (kcal) **410**

Carbohydrates (g) **12**

Protein (g) **15**

Fat (g) **20**

Ingredients

1 avocado
80g peas, cooked
juice of ½ lemon
5 fresh mint leaves, finely chopped
50g goat's cheese
2–4 slices wholegrain bread
2 tbsp hemp seeds
pea shoots (optional)

Supplying 16g of protein per serving, this quick, tasty recipe is great for a post-workout meal when you're short on time. I would always opt for wholemeal bread after exercise to ensure my carbohydrate intake is of good quality. Seeds are also an easy way to increase plant-based protein intake; this recipe uses hemp seeds, but you can swap for sesame, sunflower or flax seeds as you like.

1 Add the avocado flesh, peas, lemon juice, mint leaves and 40g of the goat's cheese to a blender and blitz until smooth.
2 Toast the bread and top with the avocado mixture, crumble the remaining cheese on top and scatter the seeds and pea shoots (if using) over to serve.

Baked sweet potato chilli

Fitness

Pregnancy
and fertility

Serves 2

Prep: 10 minutes

Cook: 40 minutes

Nutrients per serving

Kcal **650**

Carbohydrates (g) **44**

Protein (g) **67**

Fat (g) **24**

Ingredients

2 sweet potatoes
1 tbsp coconut oil
4 spring onions, diced
400g lean beef mince
2 tsp smoked paprika
1 tsp ground cumin
1 tsp cayenne pepper
200g tinned kidney beans, drained
   and rinsed
400g tinned chopped tomatoes
200ml beef stock
cottage cheese
Fresh coriander, to serve (optional)

Not only a great source of carbohydrate, sweet potatoes also provide copper, which can help maintain healthy muscle tissue and replenish energy levels and vitamin C, which helps prevent muscle breakdown. If you don't like beef, swap it for minced chicken, pork or turkey. This is a tasty post-workout meal that can be enjoyed immediately or prepped ahead of time and reheated. For extra protein, serve with a dollop of cottage cheese.

1   Preheat the oven to 220°C/200°C fan/gas mark 7. Prick the sweet potatoes all over with a fork and wrap them loosely in tinfoil. Bake until tender (about 40 minutes).

2   In a large pan melt the coconut oil over a medium heat. Add the spring onions and minced beef and cook, stirring, for about 4 minutes. Once the meat is browned add the spices, kidney beans, tinned tomatoes and beef stock. Bring to the boil and stir for 1 minute. Simmer, uncovered, for 10–15 minutes.

3   Split open the sweet potato and top with the chilli, a spoonful of cottage cheese and some fresh coriander, if desired.

Quinoa veggie burger with roasted red pepper relish

Fitness

Hormonal health

Vegetarian

Makes 6 burgers

Prep: 10 minutes

Cook: 20 minutes

Nutrients per serving

Calories (kcal) **190**

Carbohydrates (g) **30**

Protein (g) **9**

Fat (g) **3**

Ingredients

3 tbsp coconut oil
4 cloves garlic, minced
1 small onion, finely chopped
1 small carrot, finely chopped
handful of rocket, finely chopped
350g quinoa, cooked
60g breadcrumbs
2 tbsp dried oregano
1 egg
400g cannellini beans, rinsed, drained and mashed
salt and pepper

For the relish:

1 tsp cumin
2 tbsp lemon juice
2 red peppers, roasted and finely chopped
1 tbsp honey
½ onion, minced
6 burger buns, toasted, to serve (optional)

Quinoa is a versatile grain that provides a decent amount of plant-based protein. These burgers are full of colour, flavour and texture and packed with antioxidant-rich vegetables. You can add whatever toppings you like and serve with salad, pitta pockets or brioche buns, which are well earned after a tough workout! You can freeze the individual burgers for up to one month. Thaw in the fridge and then cook as needed.

1 Heat 2 tbsp coconut oil in a pan over a medium heat. Add the garlic, onion and carrot and cook until soft, about 7–8 minutes. Transfer to a bowl and add the rocket, quinoa, breadcrumbs, oregano, egg and mashed beans. Season with salt and pepper.

2 Divide the mixture into 6 burgers, place on a plate and refrigerate for 20 minutes to stiffen up.

3 To make the red pepper relish, combine all the ingredients in a small bowl and cover with clingfilm. Let it sit for 20 minutes while the burgers are chilling.

4 Heat the remaining 1 tbsp of coconut oil in a skillet over a medium-high heat, add 2 burgers at a time to the skillet and cook on each side for 4 minutes or until well browned on both sides.

5 Serve on toasted burger buns, if desired, topped with relish and any other toppings you like. A poached egg goes nicely on top!

Hummus-crusted chicken with zesty lemon quinoa

Fitness

Cognitive health

Immune health

Serves 2

Prep: 10 minutes

Cook: 25 minutes

Nutrients per serving

Calories (kcal) **610**

Carbohydrates (g) **60**

Protein (g) **75**

Fat (g) **20**

Ingredients

1 tbsp olive oil
1 yellow pepper, sliced
1 aubergine, chopped
1 tsp smoked paprika
100g hummus
2 boneless, skinless chicken breasts
1 lemon
240ml chicken stock
120g quinoa
1 cucumber, sliced
50g feta, crumbled
salt and pepper

When I came up with this recipe, I didn't expect the hummus to bring much to the dish, but it really does add a lovely flavour and texture. It is also an excellent source of plant-based protein. You can make your own hummus at home or use your favourite shop-bought hummus – plain, sundried tomato, beetroot or caramelised onion. This is great in a work lunchbox or as an on-the-go meal.

1 Preheat the oven to 200°C/180°C fan/gas mark 6. Brush a little oil on two baking trays. In a large bowl toss together the sliced pepper and chopped aubergine with the olive oil, a pinch of salt and pepper and the smoked paprika. Spread the vegetables on one of the baking trays.

2 Put the chicken breasts on the other baking tray and cover them evenly with hummus. Squeeze the lemon (keeping a little lemon juice for later) over both the vegetables and the chicken breasts, then thinly slice the squeezed lemon and place the slices between and around the chicken breasts.

3 Bake the vegetables and chicken in the oven for 25 minutes, until the chicken is cooked through.

4 Meanwhile, make the quinoa. Bring the chicken stock to the boil, add the quinoa and cover with a lid. Simmer on a medium heat for 20–25 minutes. Check halfway through and add a little water if the quinoa is looking dry. When the quinoa is cooked, stir in the remaining lemon juice and add the chopped cucumber and crumbled feta.

5 Top the quinoa with the vegetables and the hummus-coated chicken. Serve warm or seal in an airtight container and consume within two days.

Creamy chicken stroganoff

Fitness

Heart health

Pregnancy and fertility

Serves 4

Prep: 5 minutes

Cook: 20 minutes

Nutrients per serving

Calories (kcal) **530**

Carbohydrates (g) **35.5**

Protein (g) **39.5**

Fat (g) **16.5**

Ingredients

240g wholewheat noodles
2 shallots, diced
2 tbsp coconut oil
450g chicken mince
1 tbsp dried thyme
2 tsp smoked paprika
3 tsp garlic powder
salt and pepper
400g button mushrooms,.sliced
2 tbsp plain flour
600ml chicken stock
300g Greek yoghurt

This one-pot recipe is a healthy take on the classic stroganoff dish. Smart swaps include using Greek yoghurt instead of sour cream and opting for wholewheat noodles, which provide fibre for digestive and heart health. The dish is also a good source of protein, B vitamins and vitamin D, and offers a good serving of calcium.

1 Cook the noodles according to the instructions on the packet.
2 Meanwhile, sauté the shallots in the coconut oil in a large skillet over a medium-high heat until browned, about 3–4 minutes.
3 Add the chicken mince, thyme, smoked paprika, garlic powder and a pinch of salt and pepper. Cook for 4–5 minutes until the chicken is browned, breaking up the meat with a spoon as it cooks.
4 Add the sliced mushrooms and continue to cook until the mushrooms begin to soften, about 5–6 minutes. Sprinkle over the flour to coat the chicken and mushrooms and stir for 1 minute.
5 Add 200ml of stock at a time, stirring after each addition. Add the cooked egg noodles and Greek yoghurt and heat through.

Comforting sweet potato cottage pie

Fitness

Heart health

Pregnancy and fertility

Serves 4

Prep: 40 minutes

Cook: 20 minutes

Nutrients per serving

Calories (kcal) **500**

Carbohydrates (g) **42**

Protein (g) **30**

Fat (g) **23**

Ingredients

2 tbsp coconut oil
500g lean beef mince
650g sweet potatoes, peeled and chopped into large chunks
75ml milk
1 onion, diced
1 garlic clove, minced
1 celery stick, finely chopped
1 carrot, finely chopped
200ml tomato passata
100ml beef stock
1 tbsp Worcestershire sauce
grated cheese (optional)

Cottage pie is such a comforting midweek dinner and I love the sweet potato topping in this recipe. I make it in batches and store it in the freezer to have during the week. You can serve it with cottage cheese for an extra protein hit – 110g of cottage cheese contains around 14g of protein. This recipe uses lean beef mince, but you could use chicken, turkey or pork mince instead.

1 Preheat the oven to 200°C/180°C fan/gas mark 6.
2 Heat 1 tbsp of coconut oil in a large frying pan over a high heat. Add the beef and fry, breaking up the meat, until browned. Transfer the cooked meat to a plate and set aside.
3 Bring a large saucepan of salted water to the boil and add the sweet potato chunks. Simmer uncovered for 10–12 minutes or until tender. Drain, return to the saucepan with the milk and mash until smooth.
4 While the potatoes are cooking, heat another tbsp of coconut oil in the frying pan, add the onion, garlic, celery and carrots and fry for 5–6 minutes. Add the passata and the beef stock and simmer for 5 minutes. Add the beef mince, bring to the boil and simmer for 20 minutes.
5 Remove from the heat and stir in the Worcestershire sauce, then spoon the mixture into a large baking dish and top with the mashed sweet potato.
6 Bake in the oven for 20 minutes, adding grated cheese for the final 10 minutes of cooking if you wish. Serve warm. Sealed leftovers will keep in the fridge for 3 days.

Spinach and ricotta fusilli

Fitness

Bone health

Cognitive health

Vegetarian

Serves 2

Prep: 5 minutes

Cook: 15 minutes

Nutrients per serving

Calories (kcal) **380**

Carbohydrates (g) **56**

Protein (g) **36**

Fat (g) **14**

Ingredients

150g chickpea fusilli or
   wholewheat spaghetti
1 tbsp olive oil
2 garlic cloves, minced
200g spinach
125g ricotta
juice of ½ lemon
1 tbsp grated Parmesan (optional)
pepper

I don't think anyone needs an excuse to have pasta for dinner. It's so comforting, satisfying and delicious! This recipe is a perfect post-workout refuel: ricotta cheese contains whey protein to support muscle protein synthesis after exercise. This dish comes together in minutes and is made with chickpea fusilli, a higher-protein option than other pasta families. Minimal ingredients for a simple, quick, delicious midweek meal.

1 Cook the pasta according to the package instructions until al dente. Drain, reserving a small cup of the cooking water.
2 Add 1 tbsp olive oil to a large frying pan and fry the garlic for 2–3 minutes over a medium heat. Add the spinach, ricotta, lemon juice, the reserved pasta water and season with a pinch of pepper.
3 Add the drained pasta to the pan and stir well to combine. Sprinkle with grated Parmesan, if desired.

Five-minute no-bake protein bars

Fitness

Gut health

Vegetarian

Makes 12 bars

Prep: 5 minutes, plus 30 minutes in the fridge

Nutrients per serving

Calories (kcal) **210**

Carbohydrates (g) **23**

Protein (g) **12**

Fat (g) **8.5**

Ingredients

220g rolled oats
2 scoops protein powder of choice
200g almond butter
100ml maple syrup
100g dark chocolate, melted
Toppings of choice, e.g. bee pollen, coconut flakes, chopped nuts, goji berries

Whey protein is an easy way to increase protein intake, and it can be easily incorporated into baking. These bars take only 5 minutes to whip up and use minimal ingredients, so are one of my go-to recipes to have stored in the fridge or freezer. I like to cover them with dark chocolate and goji berries, but you could top them with coconut flakes, pecans, bee pollen ...

1 Line a 20 x 20 cm baking tin with baking paper.
2 Mix together the rolled oats and protein powder in a large bowl.
3 In a Pyrex bowl over a pot of simmering water, gently melt the almond butter and maple syrup and mix until combined.
4 Combine the wet ingredients with the dry ingredients and mix well. Transfer the mixture into the baking tray, top with melted dark chocolate and toppings of your choice, if desired, and refrigerate for at least 30 minutes before slicing.

Chocolate protein pudding

Fitness

Vegetarian

Serves 1

Prep: 10 minutes

Nutrients per serving

Calories (kcal) **170**

Carbohydrates (g) **17**

Protein (g) **15.5**

Fat (g) **3**

Ingredients

80ml milk of your choice
1 tbsp cacao powder
1 tbsp maple syrup
4 egg whites

Egg whites are a complete protein source – they contain all the essential amino acids that the body needs to build and repair muscle tissue. The protein in egg whites is quickly absorbed by the body, making it an ideal food for post-workout recovery. This is a delicious and satisfying post-workout treat which you can store easily in the fridge.

1 Whisk together the milk, cacao powder and maple syrup in a pan over a low to medium heat until the milk starts to bubble.
2 Pour in the egg whites and simmer the mixture, whisking, for 4–5 minutes or until it has thickened. Remove from the heat and transfer to a bowl.
3 Blend the mixture with a handheld mixer or in a blender until smooth. Cover the bowl with clingfilm and refrigerate for 1 hour before serving.

Immune health

Our immune system is made up of organs, cells and proteins that work together to protect us from bacteria, viruses, fungi and toxins. The immune system can be divided into two distinct parts:

1 **The innate immune system:** Innate or nonspecific immunity protects us against all antigens or 'invaders' and it is the defence system we are born with. You can think of it as a rapid response system and the first line of defence. It is made up of the skin, the cornea and the mucous membrane that lines the gastrointestinal, genitourinary and respiratory tract. When this system recognises an antigen, it responds instantaneously. The cells of the immune system surround and cover the antigen and it is killed in a process known as phagocytosis. This is a rapid, non-specific response to any foreign body. For example, if you get a papercut, white blood cells will rush to the site to prevent an infection.

2 **Acquired or adaptive immunity:** This is our second line of defence. It is specific to the type of pathogen it is dealing with. It is regulated by cells and organs of the body like the spleen, bone marrow, thymus and lymph nodes. When a foreign substance like a virus enters the body, antibodies are created, and immune cells multiply that are specific to that harmful substance and work to attack and destroy it. Our immune system then adapts and learns to recognise that foreign substance so that if it enters the body again our system can attack and destroy more quickly and efficiently. Our adaptive immune response should attack non-self pathogens, but sometimes it can actually attack itself and this is how many autoimmune conditions can develop like rheumatoid arthritis or lupus. While the innate response is rapid, the adaptive response is not, but the effect is long-lasting, highly specific and is sustained by memory T cells.

What factors decrease immunity?

So, immunity is our body's defence system – its protection against pathogens or infectious disease. Some factors can lower our body's defences, however, and make us more susceptible to illness. Some of these include:

• **Inflammation:** This is a natural and normal process of our immune response. It can generate pain, swelling and a release of fluids to help flush out pathogens. Pathogens are micro-organisms that can cause disease. They include viruses, bacteria, fungi and parasites. Some level of inflammation is good as the release of histamine associated with inflammation causes the release of more white blood cells to fight infection. The acute inflammation that occurs if you do something like sprain your ankle is helpful as it brings blood flow and immune cells to the area in order to heal and recover. However, chronic inflammation can lead to tissue damage and can overwhelm the immune system. Chronic inflammation has been linked to conditions like PCOS (polycystic ovary syndrome), heart disease, autoimmune conditions and diabetes. Poor nutrition choices, stress, lack of movement or too much exercise and exposure to toxins can contribute to chronic inflammation.

- **Ageing**: As we age, our immune-related organs like the thymus or bone marrow may produce fewer of the immune cells needed to fight infections. There may also be a diminished function of these cells, and as a result older people may not respond as robustly to pathogens as the young.

- **Obesity**: Excess weight is linked to low-grade chronic inflammation. Fat tissue produces what are known as adipocytokines, which can promote inflammation. Some research also points to impaired function of T cells in people who are obese. T cells are a type of white blood cell that are responsible for recognising and attacking specific antigens, which are proteins found on the surface of cells or viruses that trigger an immune response.

- **Chronic stress**: A hormone called cortisol, which is released when we feel stressed, suppresses inflammation, which is initially needed to activate immune cells.

- **Lack of sleep**: Studies have shown that people who do not get adequate restorative sleep are more likely to get sick after being exposed to a virus such as the common cold. In addition, lack of sleep can also affect how quickly we recover after infection. Sleep contributes to both innate and adaptive immunity. Certain types of cytokines that are needed for immune responses are produced when we sleep. Given the importance of sleep for the immune system, making it a priority to get a sufficient amount of good-quality sleep can work to strengthen immune function.

- **Poor diet**: A diet high in sugar, saturated fat and highly processed foods can negatively impact immune health. A poor diet can be lacking in:

  - **Vitamin C**: This antioxidant vitamin plays a vital role in maintaining the integrity of the skin, which is the first line of defence against pathogens. It also supports the production of white blood cells, which are essential for fighting infections.

  - **Vitamin D**: Helps regulate the immune system by modulating the function of T cells. It also plays a role in the production of antimicrobial peptides, which are natural antibiotics that help protect against infections.

  - **Vitamins A and E**: These antioxidant vitamins help protect the body against oxidative damage and support the function of the immune system.

  - **Zinc**: This mineral is necessary for the development and function of immune cells. It also plays a role in wound healing and maintaining the integrity of the skin.

  - **Selenium**: This antioxidant mineral supports the immune system by helping to prevent oxidative damage to cells. It also plays a role in the production of antibodies, which are proteins that help fight infections.

  - **Iron**: Important for the production of red blood cells, which carry oxygen to tissues and organs, including the immune system. It also supports the function of immune cells.

Can we boost our immune system?

We often see diets or supplements offering to 'boost' the immune system. However, this is not something we actually want to do! Overactive immune responses are what lead to autoimmune conditions. We don't want to boost our immune system, but we want it to be balanced.

So, how can we keep our immune system in balance?
- **Aim to be physically active for around 150 minutes per week**
- **Limit or reduce stress**
- **Aim for 7–8 hours of good-quality sleep per night**
- **Quit smoking**
- **Eat a balanced diet**

A balanced diet can support immune health

It is unlikely that one specific food offers special protection from infection, but eating a wide range of nutrients as part of a varied diet is essential for the health and function of all bodily cells, including immune cells.

Micronutrients

The immune system is a complex network, which requires micronutrients at every stage of the immune response. In relation to innate immunity, micronutrients play important roles in maintaining the functional and structural integrity of physical barriers like the skin. Micronutrients also support the activity of antimicrobial proteins. Deficiencies of micronutrients can impact both innate and adaptive immunity and can contribute to immunosuppression which in turn can increase the susceptibility to infections.

Vitamin A
- Vitamin A is found in liver, eggs and dairy products.
- Provitamin A carotenoids are found in foods like carrots, spinach and orange fruits and vegetables.
- An essential micronutrient for immunity.
- Helps to maintain the integrity of epithelial tissues and mucus membranes – the body's first line of defence against pathogens.
- Involved in secreting pro-inflammatory cytokines.
- Involved in the production of antibodies.
- Plays a role in the activity of macrophages.
- Stimulates the production and activity of white blood cells.
- One of the first symptoms of vitamin A deficiency is night blindness as vitamin A plays an important role in vision.

Vitamin B2 (riboflavin)
- Found in dairy, eggs, lean beef and pork, chicken, salmon, almonds and spinach.
- A micronutrient with antioxidant and anti-inflammatory functions.
- Bacteria in our gut can produce small amounts of B2 but not enough to meet dietary requirements.
- A deficiency can cause symptoms like cracked lips, sore throat, hair loss and a swollen tongue (glossitis).

Vitamin C
- Food sources include citrus fruits, leafy green vegetables, potatoes, strawberries, tomatoes, broccoli, Brussels sprouts and green and red peppers.
- Breast milk is an adequate source of vitamin C for newborns and infants.
- Fruits and vegetables can lose their vitamin C concentration through processing (such as heating) or being stored for long periods of time, so eat them soon after purchasing and consider steaming as an option to limit nutrient loss.
- An essential micronutrient and potent

antioxidant that supports cellular functions of both the innate and adaptive immune systems.
- Essential for growth and repair of tissue all over the body.
- In relation to the common cold, taking a vitamin C supplement has not been shown to prevent colds, but some studies have found that it can decrease the length of symptom duration.
- Enhances the absorption of non-haem iron (the type found in plant-based foods).

Vitamin D
- Vitamin D is available in two forms: D2 and D3. Vitamin D2 is made from plants and is found in fortified foods and some supplements. Vitamin D3 is produced naturally by the body and is found in animal foods. There is still an ongoing debate regarding which form is superior, but it appears that vitamin D3 (cholecalciferol) is better at raising blood concentration levels of vitamin D than vitamin D2 (ergocalciferol).
- A fat-soluble vitamin that is mainly made in the skin after exposure to ultraviolet (UV) rays from sunlight (in the form of D3).
- To a lesser extent it is derived from food sources like fatty fish, fish oil, cheese and egg yolks.
- In Ireland people aged 12–65 should take a 15mcg (micrograms) or 600IU (international unit) vitamin D supplement from October to March. Children aged 5–11 years require a supplement of 10mcg (400IU).
- Produces antimicrobial proteins and has anti-inflammatory properties.
- Immune cells have vitamin D receptors, which means that they require vitamin D in order to be activated and do their jobs.
- Deficiency in vitamin D is associated with increased susceptibility to infection as well as autoimmunity.

- Symptoms of vitamin D deficiency may include fatigue, loss of appetite, muscle weakness and depression or feelings of sadness, as well as getting sick more easily.

Zinc
- Dietary sources include meat, fish, eggs, dairy, whole grains, nuts and legumes.
- Zinc from animal sources has higher bioavailability than zinc from plant-based sources.
- Vegans and vegetarians are more likely to be deficient as meat is a good source of zinc. In addition, compounds called phytates, contained in grains and beans, can reduce the amount of zinc the body absorbs.
- Zinc is an essential trace element that plays a key role in regulating the function of both the innate and adaptive immune system.
- Helps to decrease oxidative stress.
- Antiviral effects.
- Maintenance of membrane barrier integrity.
- Limits the overproduction of inflammatory cytokines.
- Zinc deficiency may manifest in slow growth, diarrhoea and loss of appetite in infants and children. At any age it can cause a loss of taste and smell and can delay wound healing.

Selenium
- Good sources of selenium include oysters, Brazil nuts, halibut, tuna, eggs, sunflower seeds and shiitake mushrooms.
- Selenium is an essential mineral that must be obtained from our diet.
- It acts as an antioxidant by preventing cell damage caused by free radicals.
- Selenium may lower markers of inflammation in the body.
- Some studies have shown that increased blood levels of selenium are associated with enhanced immune response.

Iron

- Food sources include red meat, dark green leafy vegetables like kale and spinach, nuts, kidney beans, chickpeas and lentils.
- Iron is fundamental to the healthy development of the immune system. Iron deficiency degrades non-specific immunity, your body's first line of defence.
- Women (who need more iron than men) require even more during pregnancy.
- Vegetarians and vegans can struggle to meet iron requirements as our body finds it more difficult to absorb non-haem (plant-based) iron than haem (animal-based) iron.
- Tea, coffee and dairy products in high amounts can reduce the absorption of iron. Vitamin C can help with the absorption of non-haem iron.

Protein

- Protein is a macronutrient that plays an important role in immune function.
- Amino acids are essential for the synthesis of immune proteins like cytokines and antibodies.
- Some studies have shown that a diet lacking in protein can impair immune function and increase susceptibility to infectious disease.

The microbiome

The microbiome is the community of micro-organisms, including bacteria, viruses and fungi, that live within the human body. These micro-organisms are found in many different parts of the body, including the gut, skin and reproductive tract. The microbiome helps with digestion, produces vitamins and plays an important role in immune function. Imbalances or disruptions in the microbiome have been linked to a range of health conditions, including obesity, mental health disorders and autoimmune conditions.

- Our microbiome plays a pivotal role in immune function.
- Our gut is a major site of immune activity, with over 70 per cent of immune cells residing there.
- Antimicrobial proteins are also produced in the gut.
- Our diet plays a role in determining what type of microbes inhabit our guts. A diet rich in fibre and plant-based foods, whole grains and legumes appears to support the growth of beneficial or friendly bacteria. Certain friendly bacteria break down fibre into short-chain fatty acids, which have been shown to stimulate immune cell activity. These fibres are referred to as prebiotics, as they feed microbes.
- Probiotic foods contain helpful live bacteria and prebiotic foods contain fibre that feeds and maintains the functioning of those helpful bacteria.
- Probiotic foods include yoghurt, kimchi, kombucha, sauerkraut, miso, tempeh and kefir.
- Prebiotic foods include onions, asparagus, leeks, bananas, garlic and seaweed.

Keep in mind

Everyone is unique and the best nutritional advice is not a one-size-fits-all approach. Focusing on your individual needs based on your gender, age, weight and health status is important. The information provided here is simply that – information you can use in order to build a balanced and varied diet that suits your individual needs and lifestyle.

Caramelised banana porridge

Immune health

Gut health

Hormonal health

Pregnancy and fertility

Vegetarian

Serves 1

Prep: 2 minutes

Cook: 10 minutes

Nutrients per serving

Calories (kcal) **350**

Carbohydrates (g) **65**

Protein (g) **7**

Fat (g) **5.5**

Ingredients

1 tbsp coconut oil
1 tbsp maple syrup
1 banana, sliced
50g jumbo oats
250ml milk of choice
1 tsp ground cinnamon
1 tbsp manuka honey
chopped hazelnuts, to serve

This is a recipe that gets me out of bed in the morning. It's refined sugar-free but has a gorgeous sweetness thanks to the caramelised banana and manuka honey. Bananas are a source of prebiotics that feed our friendly bacteria, and oats are a great source of fibre, helping us feel full all morning while sustaining blood sugar levels. For a probiotic boost, serve with a helping of live yoghurt.

1 Melt the coconut oil in a frying pan over a medium-high heat. Add the maple syrup and when it starts sizzling, add the sliced bananas. Cook on each side for about 5 minutes until golden brown.

2 While the bananas are cooking, put the oats and milk in a saucepan and bring to the boil. Reduce the heat to low, add the cinnamon and manuka honey and simmer until thickened.

3 Pour the porridge into bowls and top with the caramelised banana and chopped hazelnuts.

Chicken noodle soup

Immune
health

Cognitive
health

Gut health

Hormonal
health

Serves 2

Prep: 10 minutes

Cook: 30 minutes

Nutrients per serving

Calories (kcal) **265**

Carbohydrates (g) **29**

Protein (g) **26**

Fat (g) **3**

Ingredients

1l chicken stock
1 boneless, skinless chicken breast
1 garlic clove, finely chopped
1 tbsp olive oil
1 onion, finely chopped
1 carrot, chopped
1 celery stalk, chopped
½ tsp dried thyme
50g wheat or rice noodles
2 tsp soy sauce
40g sweetcorn

As a child, when I was unwell, Mum would cook chicken noodle soup. It is light, easy on the stomach and provides fluids and electrolytes to prevent dehydration, which can occur alongside a fever. Chicken provides protein and zinc; carrots provide vitamin A and there is a decent amount of vitamin C from celery and onions. It is a delicious at any time, but particularly soothing when you're feeling poorly.

1 Pour the stock into a large pan and add the chicken breast and garlic. Bring to a boil, then reduce the heat and simmer for 20 minutes or until the chicken is tender.

2 While the chicken is cooking, add 1 tbsp of olive oil to a frying pan over a medium heat and add the onion, carrot and celery. Cook for 5–6 minutes until the vegetables have softened, and then add the thyme and stir for a further minute.

3 When the chicken is cooked, remove from the pot and shred with two forks. Add the chicken back to the pan along with the noodles, vegetables, soy sauce and sweetcorn. Simmer for 4–5 minutes until the noodles are tender.

Cheddar, onion and asparagus frittata

Immune health   Bone health   Fitness   Vegetarian

Serves: 4

Prep: 10 minutes

Cook: 15 minutes

Nutrients per serving

Calories (kcal) **195**

Carbohydrates (g) **2**

Protein (g) **16**

Fat (g) **13**

Ingredients

1 tbsp olive oil
1 small onion, chopped
8 eggs, beaten
1 tsp dried oregano
50g Cheddar cheese, grated
100g asparagus tips

A frittata is great when you want something warm for breakfast but don't have much time. You can make it ahead and reheat it in the oven. This recipe is packed with the vitamins, minerals and phytonutrients your body needs to support a healthy immune system. Oregano contains antioxidants that can support the immune system, and you can add extra herbs and spices. Serve with sourdough for a gut-loving helping of fermented food.

1 Heat the olive oil in a large frying pan and add the onion. Cook for 7–8 minutes until softened.
2 In a bowl, mix together the eggs, oregano and 25g of the cheese. Pour the mixture over the onion in the pan and then scatter over the asparagus tips.
3 Top with the remaining cheese and place under a hot grill for 5–6 minutes until cooked through. Cut into wedges and serve or store in the fridge in an airtight container for three days.

Halloumi and broccoli salad

 Immune health

 Bone health

 Cognitive health

 Skin health

 Vegetarian

Serves: 4

Prep: 15 minutes

Cook: 15 minutes

Nutrients per serving

Calories (kcal) **305**

Carbohydrates (g) **11.5**

Protein (g) **15**

Fat (g) **23**

Ingredients

100g hazelnuts, roughly chopped
1 tbsp olive oil
400g broccoli, chopped into florets
200g cherry tomatoes, halved
250g halloumi cheese, cut into cubes

For the dressing:

1 tbsp balsamic vinegar
1 tbsp apple cider vinegar
1 tbsp honey
1 tsp dried oregano

This can be served warm or made ahead and stored in an airtight container. Sulphurous vegetables like broccoli may increase the body's production of glutathione, an antioxidant that helps in fighting oxidative stress. Glutathione may also improve the activity of natural killer cells, which respond to cells that are infected with a virus. Hazelnuts are a great source of antioxidant-rich vitamin E.

1 Preheat the oven to 200°C/180°C fan/gas mark 6. Place the hazelnuts in a single layer on a baking sheet and toast in the oven for 8–10 minutes until golden brown.
2 Add the olive oil to a frying pan over a medium heat, add the broccoli and cook for 3 minutes. Then add the halloumi and cook until golden.
3 Add the tomatoes and cook for a further 2 minutes.
4 Whisk all the dressing ingredients together in a small bowl and set aside.
5 Remove the broccoli and cheese from the pan and serve warm, drizzled with the dressing and topped with the toasted hazelnuts.

Spicy stuffed peppers

Immune
health

Fitness

Pregnancy
and fertility

Serves 4

Prep: 10 minutes

Cook: 45 minutes

Nutrients per serving

Calories (kcal) **280**

Carbohydrates (g) **13**

Protein (g) **27**

Fat (g) **12**

Ingredients

1 tbsp olive oil
1 red onion, finely chopped
2 garlic cloves, minced
500g lean turkey mince
800g tinned chopped tomatoes
1 tbsp oregano
1 tbsp Tabasco
1 tsp cayenne pepper
4 mixed bell peppers
80g grated Cheddar or mozzarella

This is such a delicious and wholesome lunch. If you don't like spice, omit the Tabasco and cayenne pepper. This recipe uses lean turkey mince, but you can use beef or chicken mince or substitute lentils to make it vegetarian. Bell peppers are an excellent source of vitamin C, and the dish is full of antioxidants and fibre.

1   Preheat the oven to 200°C/180°C fan/gas mark 6.
2   Heat the olive oil in a large frying pan over medium heat, add the onion and cook over a medium heat for 5 minutes until softened. Add the garlic and turkey and cook until the meat has browned. Add the tomatoes, oregano, Tabasco and cayenne pepper and cover with a lid. Simmer for 30 minutes.
3   Meanwhile, slice the peppers in half and scoop out the seeds. Place cut-side down on a baking tray and bake for 20 minutes until softened.
4   Once the turkey is cooked, spoon it into the peppers, sprinkle the cheese over the top and return the pepper to the oven for 8 minutes.
5   Serve warm or store in an airtight container in the fridge for 2–3 days.

Sizzling ginger sea bass

Immune health

Bone health

Heart health

Skin health

Serves 4

Prep: 10 minutes

Cook: 10 minutes

Nutrients per serving

Calories (kcal) **170**

Carbohydrates (g) **2**

Protein (g) **23**

Fat (g) **7**

Ingredients

4 sea bass fillets, skin on
salt and pepper
cooking spray oil
a thumb-sized piece of ginger,
    peeled and shredded
2 garlic cloves, thinly sliced
2 spring onions, finely chopped
4 tbsp light soy sauce
2 tbsp dark soy sauce
3 tbsp honey
1 tbsp cornflour
1 tsp sesame oil
cooked rice of your choice,
    to serve
sliced spring onion, to serve
    (optional)

Sea bass is one of my favourite fish to cook with, and it's so easy to pan fry. The key to this delicious dish is the ginger and honey glaze, which not only adds lots of flavour but has lots of immune-supporting anti-inflammatory and antibacterial properties. I like to serve it with brown rice or coconut rice, but you can opt for noodles or jasmine rice if you prefer.

1 Season the sea bass fillets with salt and pepper. Put a frying pan on a medium heat and spray with cooking oil.

2 Add the fillets skin side down and cook until the skin is golden and crisp. Flip them over and cook the other side (about 3–4 minutes on each side).

3 While the fish is cooking, put the ginger, garlic, spring onions, soy sauce, honey, 200ml water, cornflour and sesame oil in a saucepan. Whisk to combine and cook on a high heat until the sauce begins to bubble and thicken (7–8 minutes).

4 Drizzle the glaze over the fillets and serve on a bed of rice with some sliced fresh spring onion, if desired.

Lamb tagine

Immune health Fitness

Serves 6

Prep: 15 minutes

Cook: 1 hour 15 minutes

Nutrients per serving

Calories (kcal) **350**

Carbohydrates (g) **17**

Protein (g) **33**

Fat (g) **12.5**

Ingredients

1 tbsp olive oil
2 red onions, finely chopped
3 garlic cloves, minced
thumb-sized piece of ginger, grated
2 tsp ground turmeric
2 tsp ground cumin
2 tsp smoked paprika
750g lean lamb, diced
100g dried apricots
2 tbsp honey
juice of ½ lemon
400g tinned chopped tomatoes
400g tinned chickpeas, drained and rinsed
500ml chicken stock
handful of flaked almonds, to serve
salt and pepper

Lamb was never one of my favourite meats, but I love this recipe of tender lamb in a gently spiced aromatic sauce. It's also great for a dinner party. Lamb is an excellent source of iron and protein as well as vitamin B12, selenium and zinc. I like to serve this tagine with couscous and flatbreads, which can be warmed in the oven for a few minutes before serving.

1 Heat the olive oil in a large flameproof casserole dish with a lid and fry the onion over a medium heat for 5–6 minutes until softened. Add the garlic, ginger and spices and stir for a further minute.

2 Add the lamb to the pot and stir to combine, cook for 5 minutes then add the apricots, honey, lemon juice, salt and pepper, and stir again to combine.

3 Add the chopped tomatoes, drained chickpeas and stock. Bring to the boil, then reduce the heat to a gentle simmer. Cover and cook for 1 hour to 1 hour 15 minutes, or until the lamb is tender and the stew has thickened.

4 Garnish with flaked almonds and serve with warm flatbreads and couscous if desired.

Red pepper and butternut pasta

Immune health

Heart health

Pregnancy and fertility

Vegan

Serves 4

Prep: 10 minutes

Cook: 25 minutes

Nutrients per serving

Calories (kcal) **290**

Carbohydrates (g) **55**

Protein (g) **11**

Fat (g) **1**

Ingredients

1 onion, finely diced
2 garlic cloves, finely chopped
400g butternut squash, cubed
1 red pepper, chopped
400g tinned chopped tomatoes
2 tsp smoked paprika
1 tsp dried basil
220g wholewheat penne
salt and pepper

A comforting dish that contains key ingredients to support a balanced immune system. Butternut squash is a good source of vitamin A, red pepper and tomatoes are packed with vitamin C and onions and garlic contribute to antibacterial activity. It's a really easy dish to whip up and the sauce is great for sticking in the freezer.

1 Add 1 tbsp of olive oil to a large saucepan and add the chopped onion. Fry for 5–6 minutes over a medium heat until softened. Add the garlic and cook for one further minute.
2 Add in the butternut cubes, red pepper, tomatoes, paprika and basil. Add 200ml of water, cover with a lid and simmer for 20 minutes until butternut has softened. Meanwhile cook your pasta according to pack instructions.
3 Blitz the sauce in a food processor or blender to your desired consistency, season with salt and pepper to taste and serve with the pasta.

Healthy honey fruit tart

Immune
health

Fitness

Pregnancy
and fertility

Skin health

Vegetarian

Serves 8
Prep: 20 minutes

Nutrients per serving

Calories (kcal) **230**

Carbohydrates (g) **20**

Protein (g) **6**

Fat (g) **14**

Ingredients

For the crust:
15 Medjool dates, soaked in warm
    water for 10 minutes
200g cashew nuts

For the filling:
250g Greek yoghurt
2 tbsp honey
assorted fresh fruit, sliced
Toppings of your choice, e.g.
    coconut flakes, toasted flaked
    almonds, grated dark chocolate,
    pomegranate seeds, edible
    flowers

This delicious fruit tart uses a gluten-free two-ingredient crust and protein-packed Greek yoghurt. You can use whatever fruit you fancy, for example raspberries and blueberries or kiwis, strawberries and dark chocolate shavings. Greek yoghurt is a good source of probiotics, which can help support a healthy gut microbiome. Greek yoghurt and dates are both good sources of zinc, which helps to activate immune cells.

1 Line a 23cm tart tin with parchment paper.
2 Drain the dates and put them and the cashews in a food processor. Pulse until a thick dough is formed. Press evenly into the prepared tin and set aside.
3 In a small bowl, combine the honey and Greek yoghurt and mix well. Spread the yoghurt mixture evenly over the crust and decorate with fresh fruit and the toppings of your choice. Slice and serve.

Creamy tahini hummus

| Immune health | Bone health | Fitness | Heart health | Hormonal health | Vegan |

Serves 8

Prep: 5 minutes

Nutrients per serving

Calories (kcal) **150**

Carbohydrates (g) **12**

Protein (g) **6**

Fat (g) **8**

Ingredients

250g chickpeas, cooked, rinsed
    and drained
90g tahini
½ tsp ground cumin
½ tsp smoked paprika
2 tbsp olive oil
3 tbsp lemon juice
1 garlic clove, minced
4 tbsp water

This is my classic hummus recipe. I love to experiment with variations like caramelised onion, beetroot or sundried tomato, but this is the original and best. It is delicious on sourdough toast or as a dip for carrot or celery sticks. Chickpeas are a good source of plant protein and tahini contains antioxidants that can help to support the immune system and hormone balance.

1 Put all the ingredients in a high-speed blender and blend until smooth and creamy.
2 If you need to, add more water until the hummus reaches your desired consistency.

Cognitive health

From an early age we are taught that eating well helps to look after our physical health. What is sometimes not given enough attention is how food affects our mental health and well-being. In the last decade much more research has been carried out in this area and the results are fascinating.

Nutritional psychiatry is a growing discipline that focuses on the importance of food in providing essential nutrients as part of an integrated or alternative treatment for mental health conditions. Studies show that eating a Mediterranean diet can significantly impact our mental health. The Supporting the Modification of Lifestyle in Lowered Emotional States (SMILES) trial carried out in 2017 in Australia looked at the therapeutic effect of dietary changes on major depressive episodes over a three-month period. One group was randomly assigned to the diet intervention and the control group was offered social support with no dietary changes. A third of the dietary intervention group experienced full clinical remission. The degree to which people's depressive symptoms decreased largely correlated with the degree to which they improved their diet. The results reported that dietary improvement may provide an accessible treatment strategy for the management of depressive disorders. Before the SMILES trial, a number of studies had supported the theory that a diet rich in fruits, vegetables, whole grains, fish and lower intakes of highly processed foods was associated with better mental health outcomes. However, many

of these were observational studies and the importance of the SMILES trial is that it uses one of the most robust methods of quantifying data – a randomised control trial (RCT). RCTs are considered the gold standard in research when investigating causal relationships.

So what did the dietary intervention group eat? The strategy included incorporating lots of fruit and vegetables, legumes, whole grains, plant proteins, fish and healthy fats like extra virgin olive or rapeseed (canola) oil rather than saturated fats. Including fermented foods was also important. As we'll see in our gut health chapter, the more diverse our gut microbes are, the more efficient they are at making certain hormones and neurotransmitters that can contribute to our mood.

Reducing consumption of ultra-processed foods, high-sugar foods and saturated fat also improved symptoms, probably due to the reduction of chronic inflammation in the body.

Australia was the first country to use 'lifestyle medicine' – such as improving diet, physical activity and sleep, coupled with reducing smoking, stress and illicit drug use – as a foundational step in the Royal Australian and New Zealand College of Psychology clinical guidelines for the treatment of mood disorders.

These changes in lifestyle habits are not intended to replace medications, but without that platform of health all other treatments appear to be less likely to work.

The gut–brain connection and plant-based diets

The gut–brain connection refers to the bidirectional communication between the gut and the brain, which involves complex interactions between the central nervous system, the enteric nervous system and the gut microbiota. The gut and the brain are connected by the vagus nerve, a long nerve that runs from the brainstem to the abdomen and transmits signals in both directions.

Recent research has shown that the gut–brain connection plays an important role in many aspects of health, including digestion, metabolism, immune function and mental health.

Here are a few key ways in which the gut–brain connection affects mental health:

- **Neurotransmitters:** The gut–brain connection has been linked to mental health, with research showing that the gut microbiota can affect mood, stress and anxiety. The gut microbiota produces neurotransmitters such as serotonin and GABA (gamma-aminobutyric acid), which are involved in regulating mood and stress response.
- **Inflammation:** Inflammation in the gut can trigger an immune response that can affect brain function and contribute to the development of mood disorders. Chronic inflammation has been linked to the development of depression and other mental health conditions.
- **Stress response:** The gut is intimately connected with the body's stress response, and stress can affect gut function and the gut microbiota. Stress can also trigger changes in the gut microbiota that can affect mood and mental health.
- **Nutrient absorption:** The gut is responsible for absorbing nutrients from food, and imbalances in nutrient intake or absorption can affect brain function and mental health. For example, deficiencies in certain nutrients such as vitamin B12 and folate have been linked to depression and other mood disorders.

The bacteria that live in our gut are complex, but what to eat in order to maintain a healthy gut is pretty straightforward:

- **Legumes, beans and whole grains**
- **Nuts and seeds**
- **Herbs**
- **Probiotic-rich foods**

A diet higher in plant-based foods results in a more diverse collection of microbes living in our gut. The more diverse the gut, the more robust our overall health appears to be. Studies have shown this in relation to immunotherapy treatments in cancer patients and stem cell treatments. If we have a more diverse collection of microbes, we are in a better position to prevent and treat cancer.

What are ultra-processed and processed foods?

Unprocessed foods are whole foods in which the nutrients and vitamins are still intact – think of them as food in its natural state. Examples include apples, carrots and raw, unsalted nuts. These foods can be minimally processed by drying, removing inedible parts, roasting, crushing, freezing or pasteurising; these are methods used to make them more suitable to store or safer to consume.

The addition of salt, oil, sugar or other substances alters the food's natural state, for example tinned fish or fruit in syrup. Most processed foods have an extra two or three ingredients added to them.

MINIMALLY PROCESSED	PROCESSED	ULTRA PROCESSED
Tomato	Tinned tomato pasta sauce	Frozen pizza
Apple	Apple juice	Apple pie
Potato	Baked potato	Chips
Raspberries	Raspberry jam	Jammy dodgers
Wheat	Flour	Cookies

Ultra-processed foods have many other ingredients added to them, such as sugar, salt, fat, artificial colours and preservatives, which are mostly made from substances extracted from foods, like sugars and fats. Examples include frozen meals, packaged cakes and biscuits, soft drinks and fast food.

Consumption of ultra-processed foods contributes to weight gain and obesity.

A study published in the British Medical Journal (BMJ) examined dietary records of over 100,000 French adults over a five-year period and found that those who consumed ultra-processed foods had a higher risk of developing cardiovascular disease, cerebrovascular disease and coronary heart disease.

Supporting brain function through nutrition

Now let's take a look at which foods and nutrients can help to support cognitive health. Cysteine is an amino acid that has been linked to cognitive function. It is found in many protein-rich foods, both animal- and plant-based. Here are some examples of foods that contain cysteine:

- **Meat:** Beef, pork, chicken, turkey and lamb are all good source of cysteine.
- **Fish and seafood:** Tuna, salmon and prawns are rich in cysteine.
- **Eggs:** The yolk in particular is a good source of cysteine.
- **Dairy:** Cheese, milk and yoghurt are all good sources.
- **Legumes:** Lentils, chickpeas and soybeans.
- **Nuts and seeds:** Pistachios, sunflower seeds and sesame seeds in particular.
- **Whole grains:** Oats, brown rice and quinoa all contain cysteine.
- **Vegetables:** Garlic, onions, broccoli and Brussels sprouts.

Cysteine is a precursor for the synthesis of glutathione, one of the most important antioxidants in the brain. Glutathione protects the brain from oxidative stress, which can damage brain cells and impair brain function.

Cysteine is also involved in the production of several important neurotransmitters, including dopamine, norepinephrine and serotonin. These neurotransmitters are involved in mood regulation, cognition and other important brain functions.

In addition, cysteine is involved in regulating the NMDA (N-methyl-D-aspartate) receptor, which is important for learning and memory. NMDA receptors play a key role in synaptic plasticity, the ability of the brain to change and adapt in response to experience.

Overall, cysteine is an important nutrient for brain function, and its deficiency has been linked to a range of neurological disorders, including Alzheimer's disease, Parkinson's disease and schizophrenia. Ensuring adequate intake of cysteine-rich foods or supplements may help support healthy brain function.

Research shows that the best brain foods are the same ones that protect your heart and blood vessels. They include:

- **Leafy green vegetables:** Kale, spinach and broccoli are rich in vitamin K, lutein, folate and beta-carotene, nutrients found to support brain health.
- **Fatty fish:** This is an excellent source of omega-3 fatty acids, healthy unsaturated fats that have been linked to lower blood levels of beta-amyloid – the protein that forms damaging plaques in the brains of patients with Alzheimer's disease. The WHO recommends eating two portions of fish per week, but be aware of the mercury content of the fish you consume. Low-mercury options include salmon, cod, pollack and tinned tuna. Plant-based sources include avocados, flaxseeds and walnuts.
- **Berries:** The plant pigments that give berries their gorgeous colour are called flavonoids. They have been shown to help improve memory. Berries are also full of antioxidants, which help to prevent damage to cells.
- **Caffeine:** Consumed in moderation, caffeine can have many positive impacts on the brain – not that I need an excuse to enjoy my morning coffee! It has been shown to increase alertness, help concentration and improve mood and memory. Caffeine stimulates the central nervous system and promotes the release of noradrenaline, dopamine and serotonin. A safe amount of caffeine to consume is 200mg per day, but be aware that it has a long half-life and your body will take hours to metabolise and eliminate it. So if you drink coffee after midday it could affect your sleep.
- **Walnuts:** Nuts are a good source of protein and healthy fats. While no single food group is a magical preventive treatment for cognitive decline, certain nutrients in specific foods have been found to support brain health. Walnuts are high in alpha-linolenic acid (ALA). Diets rich in omega-3 ALA and other omegas have been linked to lower blood pressure. So walnuts can benefit both the heart and brain. Generally, a diet that is good for your heart is also beneficial for your brain and mood.
- **Dark chocolate:** Cacao contains a good number of antioxidants as well as plant compounds called flavonoids. A specific type of flavonoid called flavanol is found in dark chocolate and it has antioxidant and anti-inflammatory properties.

Omega-3 fatty acids

The three main types of omega-3 are ALA (alpha-linolenic acid), DHA (docosahexaenoic acid) and EPA (eicosapentaenoic acid). DHA makes up most of the total fatty acids in the brain and it is concentrated in the grey matter. The grey matter contains neurons, which allow the processing of information. Grey matter also enables the control of movement, memory and emotions. These omega-3 fatty acids are found in cell membranes, which are like a protective 'skin' that covers cells. Oily fish is a good source of omega-3 fatty acids.

Omega-3 intake is important even before we are born, particularly during the second and third trimester of pregnancy. Research has found that mothers selectively transfer DHA to their baby during pregnancy and through breastfeeding and this supports the baby's neurological development. Early cognitive

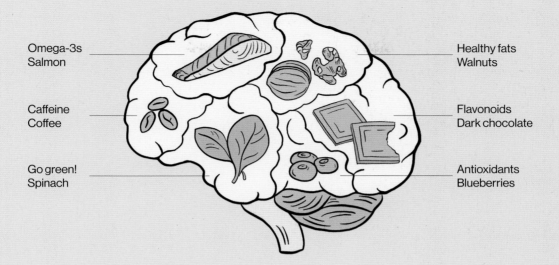

Omega-3s
Salmon

Caffeine
Coffee

Go green!
Spinach

Healthy fats
Walnuts

Flavonoids
Dark chocolate

Antioxidants
Blueberries

development in foetuses requires maternal intake of omega-3 for learning and memory. Brain cells that have higher levels of omega-3 in their membranes are thought to be better able to communicate with other cells.

While the role of omega-3 fatty acids in supporting brain function is clear, their role in various mood disorders is currently being researched. There is not enough robust evidence just yet to draw conclusions, but it appears that they may be helpful in relieving symptoms of some mood disorders such as postnatal depression.

Cognitive decline

Dementia is a general term used for loss of memory, language, problem-solving and other thinking abilities that impact quality of life. Dementia is not a single disease but rather, like heart disease, an umbrella term that covers a range of medical conditions, including Alzheimer's disease. New drug therapies

are constantly emerging for the treatment of dementia and more of an emphasis is being put on the role of modifiable risk factors in preventing the disease. Research presented at the 2019 Alzheimer's Association International Conference suggested that adopting healthy lifestyle choices like improving diet, not smoking and taking regular exercise may decrease the risk of cognitive decline and dementia.

Individual nutrients such as some vitamins, polyunsaturated fatty acids (PUFAs) and flavonoids play a role in the enhancement of cognitive performance.

Currently there are three basic dietary patterns recommended for cognitive health:
- **Mediterranean diet** – probably the most well-known, this diet is typical in Mediterranean countries and prioritises a high consumption of vegetables and other plant-based foods. It's explained more fully in the chapter on heart health.

MORE OF THESE:	LESS OF THESE:
Green leafy vegetables: every day	Red meats
Other vegetables: at least once a day	Butter and margarine
Nuts: every day	Cheese
Berries: minimum twice a week	Pastries and sweets
Beans: every other day	Fried or fast food
Whole grains: three times a week	
Fish: at least once a week	
Wine: one glass a day	
Poultry: at least twice a week	
Olive oil	

MIND diet food groups

- **Dietary approach to stop hypertension (DASH)** – designed to lower blood pressure and reduce the risk of heart disease. This diet emphasises foods that are low in saturated and trans fats, cholesterol and sodium, such as fruits, vegetables and lean protein sources. For more information, see the heart health chapter.

- **Mediterranean–DASH diet intervention for neurodegenerative delay (MIND)** – as the name suggests, this diet is an amalgamation of the Mediterranean and DASH diets, and was created to prevent dementia and loss of brain function as we age. It puts an emphasis on antioxidant-rich berry intake to support brain health, and includes ten food groups that we should eat more of and five that should be avoided or eaten in moderation.

Research continues to support the idea that dementia is not just something that happens towards the end of life but that many factors throughout our lives can affect brain health, for example cardiovascular health and nutrition. It is well documented that lifestyle changes have helped decrease death rates from cancer and heart disease, and current research is exploring if the same could be true for Alzheimer's and other dementias.

A personalised approach

From my experience of working with patients I believe that lifestyle changes need to be tailored to the individual. No two people are the same or have the same beliefs, ideas, values and experiences as each other.

Let's take a case example. It's all well and good to tell someone low in iron to take an iron supplement. You sell a high-concentration iron, which the patient might take for a week and then decides to stop because of the gastrointestinal side effects. If you take the time to listen to someone's concerns and values, you might discover that this patient reacted badly to oral iron supplements in the past, so instead you would have given a better-tolerated formulation along with dietary advice leading to a more favourable outcome.

This approach should be the same for dietary changes. Personalised dietary counselling contributes to better adherence to healthy diets. Speaking to your local pharmacist or seeking advice from a registered dietitian is one way to make a plan that suits your individual needs.

What does this mean for our daily nutrition?
Our body runs off what and how we feed it. Do you ever feel tired or sluggish after a really big meal? That's because your body is using its energy to digest that big lunch or dinner. Eating smaller portions and choosing minimally processed foods can help to combat fatigue.

Here are some tips to bear in mind:
- **Processed foods offer little to no nutritional value to the body.**
- **Choose lean proteins and fish.**
- **Choose whole grains.**
- **Snack on nuts and seeds.**
- **Increase your water intake.**
- **Add a tablespoon of chia seeds to your breakfast smoothies, yoghurt or porridge. Chia seeds are a source of prolonged energy, thanks to their carbohydrate content, healthy fats and filling fibre.**
- **Eat colourful fruits and vegetables: generally, the more vibrant and colourful the berry, the more antioxidant concentration it contains.**

The foods we eat can have a significant impact on our concentration levels. Here are some ways in which different foods can affect our ability to concentrate:
- **Carbohydrates** are the primary source of energy for the brain, and they can help improve concentration and focus. Complex carbohydrates are digested more slowly and provide a steady supply of energy throughout the day.
- **Protein** is important for the production of neurotransmitters, such as dopamine and norepinephrine, which are involved in concentration and focus. Eating protein-rich foods such as fish, eggs, chicken and nuts can help improve concentration.
- **Omega-3** fatty acids found in fatty fish such as salmon, as well as flaxseeds and walnuts, have been shown to improve cognitive function and concentration.
- **Sugar** can provide a quick burst of energy, but it can also lead to a crash in blood sugar levels and a decrease in concentration.
- **Hydration** is important: dehydration can lead to fatigue and poor concentration. Drinking enough water and staying hydrated throughout the day can help improve concentration levels.

Oaty breakfast bread

Cognitive health

Heart health

Gut health

Vegetarian

Makes 1 loaf

Prep: 10 minutes

Cook: 45–50 minutes

Nutrients per serving

Calories (kcal) **130**

Carbohydrates (g) **28**

Protein (g) **6.5**

Fat (g) **4.5**

Ingredients

380g rolled oats
2 tsp bicarbonate of soda
50ml buttermilk or milk of choice
500g plain yoghurt
1 egg
mixed seeds to top (optional)

I love having a loaf of this bread in the house; it's a handy breakfast on mornings when I'm not feeling motivated to prepare something fresh. You can add whatever toppings you like – I'd recommend peanut butter and banana slices or mashed avocado, nutritional yeast and chilli flakes. No kneading is involved, and the bread can be stored in an airtight container for up to three days.

1. Preheat the oven to 220°C/200°C fan/gas mark 7. Grease and line a 900g loaf tin with baking paper.
2. Put the oats and bicarbonate of soda in a large bowl and mix to combine. Add the buttermilk (or milk) and yoghurt and mix.
3. Lightly beat the egg in a small bowl and add this to the oat mixture. Mix everything well to form a dough.
4. Pour the mixture into the baking tin and smooth the surface over with a knife. Sprinkle with seeds (if using) and bake in the oven for 45–50 minutes.
5. Remove from the oven and allow to cool before slicing.

Butternut breakfast bowl

 Cognitive health   **Gut health**   **Immune health**   **Skin health**   **Vegetarian**

Serves 2

Prep: 15 minutes

Cook: 10–15 minutes

Nutrients per serving

Calories (kcal) **500**

Carbohydrates (g) **42**

Protein (g) **20**

Fat (g) **32**

Ingredients

half a butternut squash, spiralised or chopped into small cubes
160g kale, stems removed and leaves roughly torn
80g cherry tomatoes
extra virgin olive oil
100g quinoa
2 eggs, poached or boiled
1 avocado, sliced
40g feta cheese

For the dressing:
2 tbsp tahini paste
2 tsp miso paste
1 tsp rice vinegar
1 small garlic clove, minced
pinch each of turmeric and pepper
1 or 2 tbsp water, to thin

Anytime I go out for breakfast I order the sweet option. But on a trip to New York with my husband we found a restaurant called Jack's Wife Freda that served the most delicious breakfast bowl. It is the most energising start to the morning and serves up the protein you need for the day. If you don't have a vegetable spiraliser you can chop the butternut into small cubes.

1 Preheat the oven to 220°C/200°C fan/gas mark 7 and line a large baking tray with baking paper.
2 Place the butternut squash, kale and tomatoes on the tray with a drizzle of extra virgin olive oil. Roast for 10–15 minutes or until the kale is crisp.
3 While the vegetables are baking, cook the quinoa according to the instructions on the packet and poach or boil the eggs in a saucepan.
4 To make the dressing, combine all the ingredients in a small bowl and whisk until combined.
5 Divide the quinoa between two bowls and add the squash, kale and tomatoes. Spoon one egg into each bowl and add the avocado and crumbled feta. Pour over the dressing and enjoy.

Salmon fishcakes

Cognitive health

Heart health

Pregnancy and fertility

Serves 3-4

Prep: 20 minutes

Cook: 25 minutes

Nutrients per serving

Calories (kcal) **470**

Carbohydrates (g) **46**

Protein (g) **26**

Fat (g) **22**

Ingredients

3 salmon fillets

300g sweet potato, peeled and chopped into small cubes

1 tbsp dill, fresh or dried

1 tbsp parsley, roughly chopped

100g sourdough bread (about 2 slices)

juice of ½ lemon

1 egg, lightly beaten

1 tbsp olive oil

lemon wedges

An easy recipe that can be eaten hot or cold. Salmon is one of the richest sources of those all-important omega-3 fatty acids. If you are short on time, you can use smoked salmon – just watch out for the sodium content!

1 Preheat the oven to 200°C/180°C fan/gas mark 6. Line a baking tray with baking paper and place the salmon fillets on the tray, skin side down. Bake in the oven for 15 minutes or until the fish can be flaked with a fork.

2 Meanwhile, bring a large saucepan of water to the boil over a medium heat and add the sweet potatoes. Cook for 12–15 minutes or until the sweet potatoes are soft. Drain and mash with a fork until smooth.

3 Blitz the dill, parsley and sourdough in a food processor to form breadcrumbs.

4 Flake the salmon fillets with a fork into a large bowl. Add the mashed potatoes, lemon juice and egg and use your hands to form 4 balls. Roll them in the breadcrumb mixture, then flatten slightly to form fishcakes. Chill the fishcakes in the fridge for 15 minutes to firm up.

5 Heat the olive oil in a frying pan over a medium heat and fry the fishcakes for 2–3 minutes on each side until crisp and golden. Serve with some lemon wedges.

Tahini mango salad

| Cognitive health | Bone health | Hormonal health | Skin health | Vegetarian |

Serves 2

Prep: 10 minutes

Nutrients per serving

Calories (kcal) **390**

Carbohydrate **32**

Protein (g) **15**

Fat (g) **17**

Ingredients

30g cooked quinoa
1 carrot, sliced
1 mango, peeled and sliced
160g tofu, chopped into cubes
15g raw cashew nuts
30g feta cheese, crumbled
handful of sunflower seeds

For the dressing:

juice of ½ lemon
3 tbsp water
2 tbsp tahini
2 tbsp apple cider vinegar
1 tbsp honey

Mango is so versatile, and it can be used in both sweet and savoury dishes. It is also considered a great brain food, thanks to its vitamin B6 content. Mangoes are also a great source of minerals like magnesium, which can benefit our nervous system, mood and sleep. You can swap the tofu for another protein source – chicken, turkey or prawns work well.

1 To make the dressing, put all the ingredients in a small bowl and whisk to combine.
2 Put the quinoa, carrot, mango, tofu and cashew nuts in a large mixing bowl. Stir well to combine, pour over the dressing and top with crumbled feta and seeds. Divide the salad between two plates or store in an airtight container in the fridge for up to two days.

One-pot chicken and leek traybake

Cognitive
health

Hormonal
health

Fitness

Skin health

Serves 4

Prep: 10 minutes

Cook: 55 minutes

Nutrients per serving

Calories (kcal) **610**

Carbohydrates (g) **37**

Protein (g) **60**

Fat (g) **18**

Ingredients

cooking spray oil
4 skinless chicken breasts
1 tbsp olive oil
1 onion, sliced
4 cloves of garlic, peeled
2 leeks, sliced
200ml white wine
400ml vegetable stock
3 tsp dried thyme
600g tinned cannellini beans
200g baby spinach
400g baby potatoes, chopped into
    quarters
black pepper

This easy traybake is so easy to make and is high in iron, folate and B vitamins to support cognitive function. Leaving the skins on the potatoes ensures that you are getting a good dose of fibre to support gut health, which is closely linked to brain health. A super-easy and delicious midweek dinner that the whole family can enjoy.

1 Preheat the oven to 200°C/180°C fan/gas mark 6. Spray a large roasting tray or casserole dish with cooking spray oil and place the chicken fillets in a single layer in the dish. Set aside.

2 Add the olive oil to a large saucepan and fry the onion slices for 7–8 minutes. Add the garlic cloves and cook, stirring, for 1 minute. Add the sliced leeks and white wine and allow to bubble for 2 minutes, then add the stock.

3 Turn off the heat and add the thyme, beans, spinach and potatoes. Season with a pinch of black pepper and stir until combined. Pour the stock mixture over the chicken breasts and place in the preheated oven for 40–45 minutes, or until the chicken is cooked through.

Greek-style cod with bulgur wheat

Cognitive
health

Immune
health

Gut health

Pregnancy
and fertility

Serves 4

Prep: 10 minutes

Cook: 50 minutes

Nutrients per serving

Calories (kcal) **500**

Carbohydrates (g) **52**

Protein (g) **45**

Fat (g) **12**

Ingredients

1 tbsp olive oil, plus extra for
    greasing
1 onion, chopped
2 garlic cloves, minced
400g tinned chopped tomatoes
2 tsp smoked paprika
1 tsp chopped parsley, fresh or
    dried
4 cod fillets
50g pitted black olives, halved
200g bulgur wheat
250ml hot vegetable stock
1 tsp ground cumin
juice of ½ lemon
1 tbsp olive oil
1 spring onion, finely chopped
extra fresh parsley, chopped, to
    serve (optional)

Bulgur is one of my favourite supergrains and is often used in Mediterranean cooking. I've experimented with various ways to cook it but have settled on this method as being the easiest! Eating baked fish once a week may support brain health by reducing the amount of grey matter lost. Cod is also rich in B vitamins.

1 Add a tablespoon of olive oil to a large frying pan over a medium heat and cook the onion for 7–8 minutes. Add the garlic and cook for a further 2 minutes.

2 Add the chopped tomatoes, paprika and parsley and simmer for 10 minutes over a low heat.

3 Preheat the oven to 200°C/180°C fan/gas mark 6. Grease a casserole dish with olive oil and place the cod fillets in it in a single layer. Pour the tomato sauce over the fish and top with the olives. Cover the dish with a lid and bake for 25–30 minutes.

4 While the fish is baking prepare the bulgur wheat. Either follow the instructions on the packet or put the bulgur wheat in a large microwaveable bowl and pour in enough stock to cover. Wrap clingfilm over the bowl and place in the microwave on high for 4 minutes. Set aside to allow the bulgur to absorb the stock (about 5 minutes).

5 In a small bowl whisk together the cumin, lemon juice, olive oil and spring onion until combined and drizzle over the bulgur, mixing well to combine.

6 Remove the baked fish from the oven and serve with the bulgur and some chopped fresh parsley if desired.

Waldorf salad with prawns

Cognitive
health

Hormonal
health

Gut health

Serves 2

Prep: 10 minutes

Cook: 5 minutes

Nutrients per serving
Calories (kcal) **260**

Carbohydrates (g) **10**

Protein (g) **15**

Fat (g) **16**

Ingredients

40g walnuts
100g prawns, cooked and peeled
1 small romaine lettuce, finely
    shredded
1 celery stick, chopped
1 red apple, cored and cut into bite-
    size pieces
50g grapes, seedless, halved

For the dressing:
50g Greek yoghurt
1 tsp apple cider vinegar
1 tbsp honey
1 tbsp lemon juice
pinch of black pepper

A light and refreshing lunch option with prawns for added protein. This recipe swaps the mayonnaise that is usually used in Waldorf salad for a healthier Greek yoghurt alternative. Walnuts are a great source of omega-3 fatty acids, which are important for cognitive function and mood. Fresh fruits and vegetables are rich in antioxidants.

1 Preheat the oven to 220°C/200°C fan/gas mark 7 and line a baking tin with baking paper. Place the walnuts on the tin and roast in the oven for 5–6 minutes until toasted. Remove from the oven and allow to cool.

2 To make the dressing, combine all the ingredients in a small bowl and whisk together.

3 Divide the prawns, shredded lettuce, celery, apple chunks and grapes between two bowls, spoon over the dressing and toss to coat. Add the toasted walnuts to serve.

Brain-boosting chocolate delights

Cognitive
health

Vegan

Makes 12 slices

Prep: 15 minutes

Nutrients per serving

Calories (kcal) **170**

Carbohydrate **25.5**

Protein (g) **4**

Fat (g) **12.5**

Ingredients

240g Medjool dates, pre-soaked
in hot water for 20–30 minutes
to soften
100g walnuts
1 avocado
50g cashews
130ml unsweetened almond milk
50g coconut oil, melted
1 tsp vanilla extract
60g vegan dark chocolate chips,
melted

This recipe includes some foods that are commonly linked to brain health – avocados, walnuts and dark chocolate. These foods are rich in antioxidants and healthy fats. Although there is no magic food group to guarantee protection from cognitive decline, there is lots of research on specific nutrients that support brain function.

1   First prepare the crust by adding the dates and walnuts to a food processor. Pulse until the mixture is crumbly. Line a 20 x 30 cm baking dish with parchment paper and press the crust firmly and evenly into the dish.

2   To make the chocolate filling, put the avocado, cashews, milk, coconut oil and vanilla extract in a clean, dry food processor and blend until smooth. Add the melted chocolate and blend again until combined.

3   Pour the chocolate layer over the crust and place in the freezer for a few hours to harden.

4   Remove from the freezer and leave at room temperature for an hour before cutting into 12 slices. Store in an airtight container in the fridge for up to 4 days.

Baba ghanoush

Cognitive health

Gut health

Hormonal health

Vegan

Serves 4

Prep: 15 minutes

Cook: 10 minutes

Nutrients per serving

Calories (kcal) **114**

Carbohydrates (g**) 11**

Protein (g) **3**

Fat (g) **7.5**

Ingredients

1 large aubergine, halved
olive oil
3 tbsp lemon juice
2 garlic cloves, minced
2 tbsp tahini
2 tbsp fresh flat leaf parsley,
    chopped
¼ tsp ground cumin
salt and pepper
extra parsley, to serve

Baba ghanoush is typically served on a mezze board. Mezze means 'sharing' and a mezze board includes various cheeses, meats and dips. I am all about the dips! Hummus and tzatziki are nice, but my personal favourite is baba ghanoush. This recipe is packed with gut-loving fibre as well as vitamins B1 and B6. It goes well with chopped vegetables and pitta or flatbreads. The perfect post-study pick-me-up!

1 Heat the grill to high and lightly brush each aubergine half with olive oil. Place on aluminium foil and grill for 10 minutes. Remove and allow to cool. Scrape the flesh into a bowl and discard the skin.
2 Add the aubergine, lemon juice, garlic, tahini, parsley and cumin to a food processor and blend until creamy. Taste and adjust the seasoning as needed.
3 Serve in a small bowl with some extra chopped parsley scattered on top.

Hormonal health

When you think of hormonal health, what springs to mind? We often automatically think of life transitions such as puberty, pregnancy and menopause, but the truth is that our hormones influence every aspect of our health, both physical and mental, each and every day.

Hormones are chemical messengers that travel through the bloodstream carrying messages from the glands where they are produced to different cells in various parts of the body. I think of hormones as a switch because they are capable of turning on or turning off cellular processes that control growth, metabolism, appetite, stress, blood sugar, sexual function, sex drive, mood and sleep cycles – to name just a few!

Good nutrition is essential for the proper functioning of hormones in the body. Fibre, omega-3 fatty acids, macronutrients and micronutrients can all impact the synthesis and function of our hormones.

Seed cycling

I first heard of seed cycling when I lived in Australia. A friend of mine with PCOS (polycystic ovary syndrome) had tried different medications and supplements but wanted to support her body in a natural way. So she began seed cycling. She swore by it, she had followed it daily for about six months, and said that at last her periods had become regular again. I read up on it and was fascinated by the findings. The research is anecdotal and

more scientific evidence is needed in the area, but recent studies are looking at the benefits of seed cycling in helping to regulate our periods and also as a way to ease menopausal symptoms. While the research is in its infancy, the good news is that seeds are packed with nutrients and antioxidants, so trying it out is not going to harm your health!

It involves eating flax, pumpkin, sesame and sunflower seeds at different times of your cycle to help regulate oestrogen in the first half of the cycle and progesterone in the second half. During the follicular phase (days 1–14) you eat 1 tablespoon of ground flaxseed and 1 tablespoon of ground pumpkin seeds per day. During the luteal phase you switch to 1 tablespoon each of ground sunflower and sesame seeds. Once your period starts you go back to the flax and pumpkin seeds.

The premise is that phytoestrogens (plant compounds) can mimic the action of oestrogen. Pumpkin and flax seeds are rich in phytoestrogens and work to balance overall oestrogen levels, helping to increase or decrease oestrogen as needed. Zinc from pumpkin seeds is claimed to support progesterone production in preparation for the luteal phase. During the luteal phase the vitamin E in sunflower seeds is thought to help increase progesterone while the lignans in sesame seeds are believed to inhibit oestrogen levels from rising too high. Sunflower and sesame seeds are both rich in gamma-linolenic acid (GLA), which works to support progesterone levels and reduce inflammation in the body that may trigger PMS symptoms. (*See the recipe for Seed Cycling Granola on page 00.*)

Change the narrative

The term 'hormonal' has become synonymous with 'moody'. It is true that hormones have an effect on mood, but they do so much more in the body than that. Hormones control almost all bodily functions, from basic functions like heart rate and hunger to more complex functions like emotion and reproduction. I think we need to put more emphasis on the importance of hormones and the impact they have on our overall health.

I want to help explain hormones in a simple way in the hope that it can empower you to recognise and take action on daily habits that can positively influence your health.

The endocrine system

The body's network of hormone-producing glands and organs is called the endocrine system. Small changes in hormone levels can cause significant changes to your body and can lead to certain medical conditions that require treatment. Let's look at some of the main hormones we produce and what can happen if there is an imbalance in our bodies.

Thyroid hormones
One of the main functions of the thyroid gland is to produce hormones that help to regulate our metabolism (the process that turns food into energy). The two hormones responsible for this are called triiodothyronine (T3) and thyroxine (T4). These hormones regulate our

weight, internal body temperature, skin, hair and energy levels.

An underactive thyroid gland can result in a condition known as hypothyroidism. Common signs that your thyroid gland may not be producing enough thyroid hormones include weight gain, tiredness, sensitivity to cold, constipation and feeling depressed. Hypothyroidism is treated with a daily lifelong hormone tablet.

Hyperthyroidism, on the other hand, occurs when your thyroid gland makes too much thyroxine and this can accelerate your body's metabolism, causing unintentional weight loss, difficulty sleeping, heat sensitivity and an irregular or unusually fast heart rate.
If you believe you may be suffering with an imbalance in thyroid hormones, I advise getting your levels checked. Ask your doctor to do a blood test for TSH and T4. Unfortunately, these conditions are under-diagnosed in the community, but knowledge is power, so use this knowledge to get to the bottom of any issues you may be experiencing.

Iodine is a micronutrient that is necessary for the production of thyroid hormones. Foods rich in iodine include eggs, dairy, seafood, strawberries and cranberries.

Insulin
Insulin is released by the pancreas, and it enables the body to use glucose from carbohydrates in the food we eat for energy or to store glucose for future use. Think of it like a key that opens the door into your cells. It allows sugar (glucose) in and so regulates our blood sugar levels.

There are two main types of diabetes, which is one of the most prevalent chronic conditions

FOOD	GRAMS OF CARBS	GI RANGE	AVERAGE GI
White potato (medium)	34	56–111	High 80s
Sweet potato (medium)	24	44–78	61
Carrots (130g)	6	16–92	47
Green peas (170g)	11	39–54	48
Chickpeas (175g)	54	31–36	34
Soybeans (90g)	13	15–20	17
Apple (medium)	15	28–44	40
Banana (medium)	27	46–70	58
White bread (1 slice)	14	64–83	72
Wholewheat bread (1 slice)	12	52–87	71
Oats (45g)	27	42–75	58
Brown rice (200g)	45	39–87	66
White rice (200g)	45	43–94	72
Pasta (200g)	43	40–60	50

globally. One in ten people around the world are living with diabetes. In type 1 diabetes the pancreas no longer makes insulin, so you have to inject yourself or use an insulin pump in order to control your blood glucose levels. Type 1 diabetes tends to occur in childhood or early adult life, and it is caused by the body's own immune system attacking insulin-making (beta) cells of the pancreas.

Type 2 diabetes usually develops slowly in adulthood. If caught at an early stage, diet and lifestyle alone may be the only treatment required. Unlike type 1 diabetes, type 2 diabetes is preventable. Up to 40 per cent of diagnoses could be prevented with weight management and a healthy diet. A further 40 per cent of people may be able to delay the onset of diabetes with changes to their diet and including exercise and daily movement in their lives. Risk factors for type 2 diabetes include high blood pressure, high cholesterol, lack of

physical activity and obesity – so we can see why it is so important to modify our diet and lifestyle in order to protect our health.

What causes insulin resistance?

Obesity, other hormonal conditions such as PCOS, a diet high in high-glycaemic carbohydrates and an inactive lifestyle can all contribute to insulin resistance.

The **glycaemic index** is a rating system that grades carbohydrates according to how quickly they raise blood glucose levels. Carbohydrates with a low GI value are digested, absorbed and metabolised more slowly than high-GI foods. They typically cause a lower and slower rise in blood glucose and insulin levels.

- **Low GI: 55 or less**
- **Medium GI: 56–69**
- **High GI: 70–100**

While the GI index is helpful in highlighting

certain food groups that may spike your blood sugar levels, critics of this system point out that it does not take into account the quantity of carbohydrates you are eating. In response, the **glycaemic load** was developed. The glycaemic load is calculated by multiplying the GI value by the grams of carbohydrates eaten, and then dividing that number by 100. For example, an apple has a GI index of roughly 40 and contains 15g of carbohydrates: so (40×15)/100 = 6. The glycemic load of an apple is 6.

- **Low GL: 10 or less**
- **Medium GL: 11–19**
- **High GL: 20 or more**

Since it is carbohydrates in the food we eat that raise blood sugar an understanding of GI can help in meal planning for glucose management

Female hormones

Female hormones play a crucial role in the development and regulation of the female reproductive system and are essential for a woman's overall health and well-being. Diet can have a significant impact on female hormones, affecting everything from menstrual cycles and fertility to mood and overall health. Let's start by looking at our menstrual cycles. Periods are a completely normal and natural part of a woman's life, but society has attached a taboo to menstruation and therefore the topic is not yet openly discussed. This includes conversations around the impact of symptoms we feel when we are on our period. Recent research has found that two-thirds of women (67 per cent) experience heavy periods, but more than half of all women (55 per cent) admit that they put up with feeling fatigued and ill during their menstrual cycle because

'it's just part of being a woman'. In addition, a third (32 per cent) believe 'there is nothing that can be done to make a difference' when it comes to symptom management. I want to change that thought process and highlight that there are ways to manage symptoms.

Did you know that the leading cause of iron loss globally is menstruation? It is estimated that around one in four women in Ireland are deficient in iron, which can lead to symptoms like fatigue and not feeling yourself. Many of us think that's the norm – but it shouldn't be! Having your iron levels checked is an important step in addressing fatigue. When it comes to supplements, many women stop taking iron due to gut irritation, but there are products available that don't have these side effects, so I would always advise speaking to your GP or pharmacist.

So what are the main female hormones and what do they do?

Oestrogen

Oestrogen is mainly produced by the ovaries and plays an important role in the development of a woman's reproductive system during puberty. Oestrogen is actually a group of hormones (oestrone, oestradiol and oestriol are the main types) that help to regulate our menstrual cycle. Oestrogen also affects the liver, heart, skin and brain health and even has a helping hand in regulating metabolic processes like cholesterol levels. During the menopause, our oestrogen levels naturally decline. Hormone replacement therapy, which is now commonly prescribed by doctors, aims to replenish oestrogen levels to protect bone and heart health, alleviate poor mood and ease vaginal symptoms of menopause such as dryness.

Progesterone

Progesterone, sometimes called the 'pregnancy hormone', is an important hormone in conception. It plays a role in initiating and maintaining pregnancy by preparing the uterus to receive a fertilised egg. Progesterone is produced by the ovaries and, in pregnant women, by the placenta. This causes your body to stop ovulating and prepares the breasts to produce milk.

FSH and LH

Follicle-stimulating hormone (FSH) and luteinising hormone (LH) are released by the pituitary gland into the bloodstream. FSH stimulates the growth of ovarian follicles in the ovary. The follicle houses one egg which is released during ovulation each month. It also stimulates oestrogen production from the ovaries. LH is released during the second part of your menstrual cycle after the initial surge that causes the follicle to rupture and release a mature egg. LH is released at a constant rate for two weeks to stimulate progesterone production from the corpus luteum, formed from the ruptured follicle, in order to support pregnancy if it occurs.

A closer look at periods

The menstrual cycle can be divided into four phases:

- **Menstrual phase:** The first day of the menstrual cycle is the first day of bleeding, also known as menstruation. During this phase, the uterus sheds its lining, resulting in menstrual bleeding that lasts between three and seven days.
- **Follicular phase:** Following menstruation, the body begins to prepare for ovulation by producing follicle-stimulating hormone (FSH), which stimulates the growth and

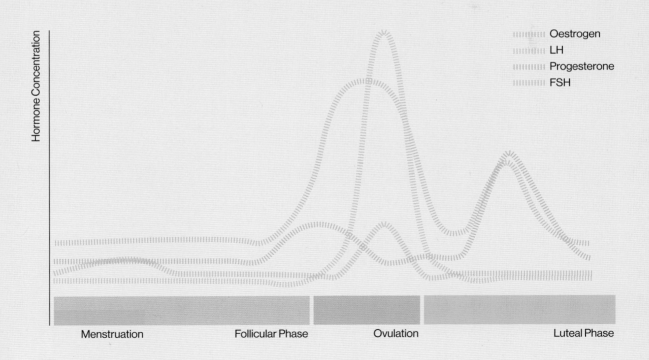

Oestrogen
LH
Progesterone
FSH

Menstruation   Follicular Phase   Ovulation   Luteal Phase development of follicles in the ovaries. These follicles contain eggs, and as they mature, they produce oestrogen, which thickens the uterine lining in preparation for implantation. The follicular phase lasts from approximately day 1 to day 14 of the cycle.

- **Ovulatory phase:** When oestrogen levels peak, they trigger a surge in luteinising hormone (LH), which causes the dominant follicle to release an egg in a process called ovulation. This typically occurs around day 14 of the cycle.
- **Luteal phase:** Following ovulation, the empty follicle transforms into a structure called the corpus luteum, which produces progesterone. Progesterone thickens the uterine lining even further in preparation for implantation. If the egg is not fertilised, the corpus luteum will degenerate, and progesterone levels will decrease, leading to the shedding of the uterine lining and the start of a new menstrual cycle. The luteal phase typically lasts from approximately day 15 to day 28 of the cycle.

Impact of diet on your hormones

Many factors can have an impact on the balance and production of hormones in the body. Some factors include:

- **Macronutrient balance:** The balance of macronutrients (carbohydrates, proteins and fats) in the diet can affect female hormones. For example, low-carbohydrate diets have been shown to increase testosterone levels, while diets high in polyunsaturated fats may decrease oestrogen levels.
- **Fibre:** Adequate fibre intake is important for healthy hormone balance. A diet low in fibre can lead to high oestrogen levels and an increased risk of breast cancer.
- **Protein:** Adequate protein intake is essential for the production of hormones. Low protein intake can lead to low levels of LH and FSH,

which can disrupt the menstrual cycle and fertility.

- **Phytoestrogens:** Certain foods, such as soy and flaxseeds, contain phytoestrogens, which can mimic the effects of oestrogen in the body. Consuming too many phytoestrogens can disrupt hormone balance, especially in women with low oestrogen levels.
- **Sugar and processed foods:** Consuming too much sugar and processed foods can lead to insulin resistance, which can disrupt hormone balance and lead to conditions such as PCOS.
- **Nutrient deficiencies:** Certain nutrient deficiencies, such as low levels of vitamin D, magnesium and zinc, can affect hormone balance and contribute to menstrual irregularities and other health issues.

Overall, a balanced and nutritious diet is essential for maintaining healthy hormone balance in women. Eating a variety of whole, nutrient-dense foods can help support healthy hormone production and regulation.

Exercise and your cycle

For women of child-bearing age, it may be beneficial to co-ordinate your workout intensity alongside your menstrual cycle. Research in this area is lacking and there are not enough robust, large-sample studies to make recommendations in this area. But from what is currently in the literature, hormone levels are low at the start of your cycle during the follicular phase, so you can prioritise high-intensity interval training, weightlifting and plyometrics with at least one day of recovery between workouts. Oestrogen is thought to have an anabolic effect on skeletal muscle and restores glycogen stores. Bear in mind that due to lower levels of oestrogen, women are at a higher risk of injury during this phase of their cycle because oestrogen helps protect against exercise-induced muscle damage and reduces inflammatory responses. Be mindful of quick changes in direction and proper knee placement during movements like lunges, squats and jumps.

After ovulation, moderate intensity and gentle movement is most beneficial. During the luteal phase, there is an increase in body temperature and fluid retention. This is also the time when PMS symptoms kick in, so listen to your body and do what feels best for you. Options include yoga, Pilates, low-intensity cardio, walking and cycling.

PMS

PMS has a wide variety of both physical and emotional symptoms. These include mood swings, food cravings, tender breasts, fatigue, irritability, acne, headaches, lower back pain and bloating. Symptoms recur in a cyclical, predictable pattern, and they tend to begin during the second half of your cycle – the luteal phase. The exact cause is unknown but hormonal changes are thought to trigger symptoms. After ovulation, the empty follicle that has nurtured the egg forms the corpus luteum, which produces high levels of progesterone. The corpus luteum degenerates if an egg is not fertilised, leading to a subsequent decline in progesterone. This decline in progesterone is believed to affect brain chemicals like serotonin.

Unfortunately, PMS and the more sinister condition of premenstrual dysphoric disorder (PMDD) are under-diagnosed. Diagnosis of PMS is based on the symptoms experienced, and to reach a diagnosis of PMS, women are encouraged to keep a symptom diary for at least two consecutive months. Usually symptoms begin after ovulation and start to ease from the first day of menstruation. If your symptoms are negatively impacting your daily life, talk to your doctor about it. The International Association for Premenstrual Disorders offer support groups, resources and online communities and assistance in finding a doctor familiar with PMDD. No woman should have to suffer in silence. Taking action will be the best thing you can do for your mental and physical health.

Treatment options

Because the exact cause is not yet understood, treatment is largely focused on lifestyle intervention. Eating a balanced diet, taking regular exercise and minimising stress, as well as limiting caffeine, alcohol and salt are all recommended treatment options. Small studies have suggested the B vitamins thiamine and riboflavin as well as vitamin D and calcium may reduce some PMS symptoms. *Vitex agnus-castus* (chasteberry) is a herbal supplement that some small studies have shown to be effective, but further research is needed in the area in order to validate the claims.

Cognitive behavioural therapy is a psychology-based intervention that some women may find beneficial for addressing emotional symptoms. In terms of medical treatment, your doctor may prescribe you one of two options – hormonal medications or selective serotonin reuptake inhibitors (SSRIs). Typically, SSRIs are used to manage depression; if they are used to treat PMS you take a tablet for just the second half of the cycle.

Here's some general advice:

- Try to eat more whole grains around five days before your period starts as this is when there is a natural drop in serotonin.
- Include lean proteins and healthy fats, which are the building blocks of all hormones, in your diet.
- Eat smaller, more frequent meals to reduce bloating.

- Sip on some ginger tea, which has anti-inflammatory properties, can soothe aching muscles and reduce nausea.
- Limit salt to reduce bloating and fluid retention.
- Try to include calcium-rich foods in your diet. If you find this difficult you could consider a supplement.
- Omega-3 fatty acids found in foods like fish, seeds and walnuts can reduce inflammation, which can help reduce period cramps.
- Make sure to stay well hydrated. Aim for two to three litres of water per day. This can ease bloating and dehydration headaches.
- Engage in at least 30 minutes of aerobic activity most days of the week. This could be a brisk walk, cycling or swimming.
- Reduce your stress levels, focus on getting enough sleep and don't take on too much. It's okay to say no to commitments – we don't always have to be busy or getting things done. take time for yourself.
- Keep a symptom diary and tracker; notice things that improve or worsen symptoms

PCOS

PCOS is a hormonal condition that can affect a woman's fertility, menstrual cycle, hormones and physical characteristics. As we've seen, during the menstrual cycle, an egg develops within a follicle in the ovary. In PCOS many follicles can develop, which can impact on or prevent ovulation. On an ultrasound they can look like a string of pearls. Symptoms include weight gain, thinning hair or hair loss from the scalp, excess facial or body hair growth, irregular or absent menstrual cycles and ovulation and oily skin or acne. These symptoms are related to abnormal hormone levels:

- **Testosterone:** The ovaries produce a small amount of testosterone in all women. In PCOS slightly elevated levels of testosterone are produced.

- **Insulin:** PCOS is often associated with insulin resistance. We know that insulin helps to move glucose into the cell so it can be used as energy. In PCOS our body stops recognising insulin, which leads to increased glucose levels. The body produces even more insulin to counteract this, which can lead to irregular periods, fertility issues and weight gain, and can also increase testosterone.

PCOS affects around 1 in 10 women in Ireland, but the condition is often overlooked and left untreated. Treatment options include anti-diabetic medications such as metformin, which helps to improve insulin sensitivity. Inositol is a non-prescription supplement that according to recent research may be effective in reducing insulin resistance, improving period regularity and reducing testosterone levels. However, more robust studies are required to prove its effectiveness.

Having PCOS increases your risk of developing type 2 diabetes and heart disease, but adjusting diet and lifestyle can play a huge role in decreasing this risk as well as improving fertility and reducing or eliminating symptoms associated with the condition.

In relation to PCOS, consulting a dietitian is an integral part of your treatment plan as the food you eat has the potential to decrease or even eliminate your symptoms. At mealtimes you want to keep three things in mind:

- **Lower inflammation:** We know that sugar can lead to inflammation in the body, so it's a good idea to keep sugar intake as low as reasonably practical. Include known anti-inflammatory herbs and spices like turmeric, and foods like berries, leafy greens and fatty fish.
- **Improve insulin sensitivity:** Since PCOS is linked to insulin resistance, eating low-GI, whole-food sources of carbohydrates may be

beneficial. Protein and fat consumption can also be prioritised. A higher-protein and lower carbohydrate plan, known as a glycaemic load plan, is a common strategy utilised for PCOS. The *American Journal of Clinical Nutrition* showed that a higher-protein diet (more than 40 per cent of calories obtained from protein) without any calorie restriction resulted in greater weight loss (17lb [7.7kg] versus 7lb [3.2kg]) in calorie-restricted diets.

- **Improve gut health:** I believe I can tie gut health and striving for a more balanced microbiome into every health condition! This is because having a balanced microbiome is linked to better health outcomes. Opt for fibre-rich and non-starchy vegetables.

Foods to focus on:

- **Natural, unprocessed foods**
- **High-fibre foods**
- **Fatty fish, including salmon, tuna, sardines and mackerel**
- **Kale, spinach and other dark leafy greens**
- **Dark red fruits, such as red grapes, blackberries, blueberries and cherries**
- **Cinnamon: 1–6g daily has been shown to decrease fasting blood sugars and improve cholesterol profiles**
- **Broccoli and cauliflower**
- **Dried beans, lentils and other legumes**
- **Healthy fats, such as olive oil, as well as avocados and coconuts**
- **Nuts, including pine nuts, walnuts, almonds and pistachios**
- **Dark chocolate, in moderation**
- **Turmeric**

Menopause

Menopause is defined as one full year after the last menstrual bleed. At this point, the ovaries stop producing oestrogen. This may cause muscles and joints to ache, bones to become more fragile and vaginal tissues to become thinner (which can lead to irritation and dryness of the vagina). Perimenopause, which can occur up to seven years before the menopause is reached, is when you start to experience menopausal symptoms, but your periods have not stopped completely: they may become less frequent over a few years before they stop completely or they can stop suddenly. In some women, periods can actually be quite heavy in the year coming up to menopause. No two women are the same and your own individual experience will be different from anyone you know, so lean into what feels good for you and your body.

Lifestyle interventions include eating a balanced and varied diet and incorporating regular exercise into your week. Weight-bearing exercise is particularly beneficial for bone and joint health. Hormone replacement therapy is now commonly prescribed to treat menopausal symptoms, so no woman has to put up with their daily life being impacted. HRT is available as a patch, tablets, gels, pessaries and sprays. Lubricants and moisturisers are also available to treat vaginal dryness.

- Flaxseeds have been linked to slight increases in oestrogen, improved hormone metabolism, fewer hot flushes, reduced vaginal dryness, and better overall quality of life in menopausal and postmenopausal women.
- Calcium-rich foods like milk, kale and yoghurt help to protect bones and prevent osteoporosis.
- Take a vitamin D supplement to help support healthy bones.
- Include omega-3 fatty acids in your diet; oily fish are the best source of omega-3s, but other sources include flaxseeds, walnuts, kidney beans, soybeans and chia seeds.

Friends and foes

Scientists have identified certain chemicals that may interfere with endocrine function, from everyday products like BPA (bisphenol A) found in some plastic bottles to phthalates found in certain cosmetics. Other common hormone disrupters include nutrient deficiencies, too much caffeine, alcohol or sugar, and stress. Because our hormones are connected, any sort of hormone imbalance can throw off other hormones. This can affect our menstrual cycles, fertility, skin, weight, brain function, mood, sleep and general well-being. The nutrients and energy we obtain through our food are the raw materials our bodies need to produce hormones. If we do not have adequate amounts of these raw materials our body will prioritise the production of our stress hormone, cortisol. Cortisol operates a negative feedback loop with endocrine glands and can 'switch off' the production of certain hormones. Have you ever noticed that during periods of high stress your menstrual cycle is delayed? This is because our body thinks we are under stress – it can't distinguish between the threat of emotional stress and the threat of physical stress, so it 'turns off' certain hormones as a survival mechanism.

A note on sugar

A diet that is high in refined sugar can increase both inflammation and insulin production in the body. As we have learnt, anything in moderation is unlikely to negatively impact our health, but when inflammation and insulin production are continuously high chronic diseases are more likely to develop. Hormonal imbalances such as gestational diabetes, PCOS, PMS and thyroid hormone imbalance are more likely to occur when there is chronic inflammation and increased insulin production. Increased insulin can also cause your ovaries to produce more testosterone, which can prevent ovulation and lead to fertility issues. If the female body has too much testosterone it can start to convert this hormone to oestrogen, resulting in oestrogen dominance, which is linked to several conditions including heavy periods, PMS, mood swings and fibroids. Too much sugar can cause our hormones to go rogue, but it's not all doom and gloom. It is never too late to start new healthy habits.

Maca chia pudding

Hormonal health | **Fitness** | **Heart health** | **Immune health** | **Vegan**

Serves 1

Prep: 5 minutes plus 2 hours/overnight chilling

Nutrients per serving

Calories (kcal) **365**

Carbohydrates (g) **36**

Protein (g) **12.5**

Fat (g) **15**

Ingredients

2 tbsp chia seeds
20g oats
250ml oat milk
1 tsp vanilla extract
1 tbsp maca powder
1 tbsp cacao powder

Adaptogens are thought to help the body adapt to and resist psychological and physical stress. One of my favourite adaptogens is maca. One tablespoon of powder contains nearly 20 amino acids, vitamins B1, B2, B12, C, and zinc, as well as calcium, fibre, iron, phosphorus and protein! Chia seeds are incredibly rich in nutrients, a source of antioxidants, fibre and omega-3 fatty acids. For added protein, layer with Greek yoghurt.

1 Add the chia seeds, oats, oat milk and vanilla extract to a jar with a lid and mix until fully combined.
2 Add the maca and cacao powder and mix again until fully combined.
3 Seal the jar and store in the fridge for a minimum of 2 hours or, for best results, overnight.

Seed cycling granola

 Hormonal health **Heart health** **Immune health** **Vegetarian**

Makes 15 servings

Prep: 5 minutes

Cook: 30 minutes

Nutrients per serving

Calories (kcal) **250**

Carbohydrates (g) **28**

Protein (g) **6g**

Fat (g) **15**

Ingredients

3 tbsp coconut oil, melted
125ml maple syrup
2 tbsp honey
1 tsp vanilla extract
300g rolled oats
50g ground flaxseed (swap for
    ground sesame seeds during
    luteal phase/after ovulation)
50g ground pumpkin seeds (swap
    for sunflower seeds during luteal
    phase/after ovulation)
100g flaked almonds
50g coconut flakes
25g dark chocolate chips

This is one of my favourite granola recipes. Not only is it quick and easy to make and packed full of nutrients, but it is also super satisfying and delicious. Good in a healthy breakfast, sprinkled over smoothie bowls or as an afternoon snack with yoghurt.

1 Preheat oven to 170°C/150°C fan/gas mark 4. Mix together the melted coconut oil, maple syrup, honey and vanilla extract in a large bowl.
2 Add in the oats and seeds and mix well.
3 Tip the granola onto two baking sheets and spread out evenly. Bake for 20 minutes, then add the flaked almonds and coconut flakes and bake for an additional 10 minutes.
4 Remove from oven and allow to cool fully. The secret to getting nice round clusters is to ensure the granola is left untouched until fully cooled. Add the chocolate chips and store in an airtight container for up to one month.

Falafel salad with tahini dressing

Hormonal health Pregnancy and fertility Skin health Vegetarian

Serves 2

Prep: 15 minutes

Cook: 15 minutes

Nutrition per serving

Calories (kcal) **250**

Protein (g) **12**

Fat (g) **8**

Carbohydrates (g) **26**

Ingredients

400g tinned chickpeas, drained and rinsed

1 onion, finely chopped

2 garlic cloves, minced

¼ bunch of fresh parsley, thick stems removed, roughly chopped

1 tsp ground cumin

pinch of chilli powder

dash of lemon juice

1 medium egg

salad leaves of choice (e.g. romaine lettuce, spinach, rocket or a mixture)

1 cucumber, sliced

2 tbsp coconut oil, melted

For the dressing:

3 pitted dates, soaked in warm water for 20 minutes, and coarsely chopped

120ml water

80ml lemon juice

60ml tahini

30g spinach

This recipe is packed with calcium, magnesium and protein as well as phytoestrogens (which can help regulate oestrogen levels). The dressing is really versatile – you can spoon it over grilled or roasted vegetables, fish or chicken or use it as a dip. Tahini is rich in zinc, copper, iron and selenium, and calcium, which helps regulate hormones. Calcium deficiency has been linked to hormone-related conditions such as premenstrual syndrome.

1 Put the chickpeas in a food processor along with the chopped onion, minced garlic, parsley, cumin, chilli powder, lemon juice and the egg, and process until finely and evenly ground.
2 Shape into round balls, using 2 tablespoons per ball.
3 Heat the oil in a large non-stick skillet over a medium heat. Cook the falafels until golden brown, approximately 5 minutes per side.
4 To make the dressing, place all the ingredients in a food processor or blender and blend until smooth and creamy.
5 Put the salad leaves and cucumber in bowls, top with warm falafels and drizzle with the dressing.

Antioxidant-rich root vegetable soup

| Hormonal health | Heart health | Immune health | Pregnancy and fertility | Vegetarian |

Serves 6

Prep: 5 minutes

Cook: 40 minutes

Nutrients per serving

Calories (kcal) **115**

Carbohydrates (g) **16**

Protein (g) **3**

Fat (g) **4**

Ingredients

2 tbsp olive oil
1 shallot, sliced
6 garlic cloves, peeled (3 minced, 3 left whole)
350g turnip, chopped
350g beetroot, chopped
350g carrot, chopped
1.4l vegetable stock
2 tbsp lemon juice
salt
2 tbsp fresh dill, chopped
cooking spray oil
200g purple sprouting broccoli
drizzle of honey

Antioxidants help the body's detoxification process by fighting cell-damaging free radicals. Root vegetables are a good source of fibre, and beetroot contains betalains, a group of phytonutrients that support liver detoxification. To top off this wholesome soup I include roasted broccoli sprouts, which contain a compound called sulphoraphane, a potent antioxidant that supports normal oestrogen balance; and glucosinolate, which supports liver detoxification and can help relieve menopausal symptoms.

1   Heat the oil in a large pan over a medium heat. Add the shallot and sauté for 4 minutes until translucent. Add the minced garlic and sauté for 1 minute longer.

2   Add the chopped turnip, beetroot, carrot, whole garlic cloves and stock. Bring to the boil, then reduce the heat to medium-low and simmer for 30 minutes. Add the lemon juice, dill and a pinch of salt and stir.

3   While the vegetables are cooking, preheat the oven to 200°C/180°C fan/gas mark 6. Spray a roasting tin with some oil and add the broccoli and a drizzle of honey and roast in the oven for 15–20 minutes.

4   Ladle the soup into a blender and blend until smooth. You may need to do this in 2–3 batches.

5   Serve warm topped with the broccoli.

Fish pie

Hormonal health   Bone health   Fitness

Serves 4

Prep: 15 minutes

Cook: 55 minutes

Nutrients per serving

Calories (kcal) **455**

Carbohydrates (g) **50**

Protein (g) **27g**

Fat (g) **15**

Ingredients

1kg potatoes, peeled and halved
400ml milk, plus extra for the mash
15g butter, plus extra for the mash
salt and pepper
20g plain flour
2 spring onions, finely chopped
200g salmon, cut into chunks
200g smoked haddock, cut into chunks
10g chives, finely chopped
handful of peas
handful of grated Cheddar cheese

Haddock is a source of omega-3 fatty acids, mostly EPA and DHA, an essential part of cell membranes. They provide the starting point for hormone production that regulates blood clotting, relaxation and contraction of artery walls, and inflammation. Salmon, halibut, mussels and anchovies contain high levels of omega-3 fatty acids. This is a family-friendly recipe that freezes well.

1 Put the potatoes in a large saucepan, cover with water and bring to the boil. Simmer for 20–25 minutes until tender, then drain and mash with a splash of milk and a knob of butter, seasoning with salt and pepper.
2 Preheat the oven to 200°C/180°C fan/gas mark 6.
3 Put the butter, flour and spring onions in a pan and gently heat until all the butter has melted, stirring constantly. Cook for 1–2 minutes. Gradually whisk in the milk, bring to a simmer and cook for 6-7 minutes or until the sauce has thickened.
4 Take off the heat and stir in the salmon and haddock, add the chives and peas, and spoon into an ovenproof dish. Top with mashed potato and sprinkle over a handful of grated cheese.
5 Cook in the oven for 20–25 minutes.

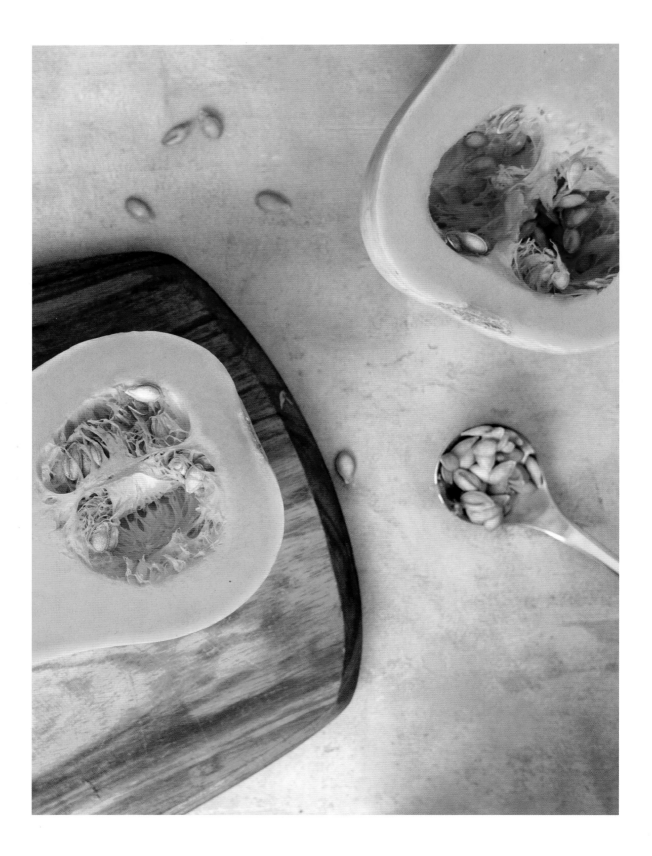

Turkey burgers with butternut boats

Hormonal health

Fitness

Gut health

Serves 2

Prep: 15 minutes

Cook: 40 minutes

Nutrients per serving

Calories (kcal) **470**

Carbohydrates (g) **26**

Protein (g) **42**

Fat (g) **39**

Ingredients

1 butternut squash, halved and deseeded
1 red onion, sliced
1 red pepper, sliced
1 courgette, sliced
1 avocado, mashed
30g spinach
2 tbsp cottage cheese

For the burgers:
250g turkey mince
1 small red onion, finely chopped
2 garlic cloves, finely chopped
1 egg, beaten
1 tsp dried oregano
1 tsp smoked paprika

What I love about these 'butternut boats' is that you can mash the flesh of the cooked butternut and add whatever you have to hand. You can eat the skin, too, with all its gut-loving fibre. Paired with these simple turkey burgers, this dish is a lean protein option incorporating healthy fats from avocado, low-GI carbohydrates, lean protein from the turkey and a healthy serving of vegetables for good measure!

1 Preheat the oven to 200°C/180°C fan/gas mark 6. Line two baking trays with parchment paper and place the butternut squash, onion, pepper and courgette on one tray. Cover with tinfoil and cook in the oven for 35–40 minutes, removing the tinfoil halfway through.

2 While the vegetables are cooking, make the burgers. Combine all the burger ingredients in a bowl and shape the mixture into two burgers around 3cm thick.

3 Put burgers on the second lined baking tray and cook in the oven for 20 minutes, turning them over halfway through.

4 Take the butternut squash and vegetables out of the oven. Allow the butternut to cool for a few minutes before mashing the flesh with a fork and topping with vegetables, avocado, spinach and cottage cheese. Serve with the burgers.

No-bake dark chocolate cashew bars

Hormonal health   Gut health   Pregnancy and fertility   Vegan

Makes 16 bars

Prep: 10 minutes, plus 6 hours chilling

Nutrients per serving

Calories (kcal) **200**

Carbohydrates (g) **22**

Protein (g) **5**

Fat (g) **12**

Ingredients

For the crust:

250g cashew nuts, soaked in water for 4–6 hours
180g organic oats
180g pitted dates
1 tbsp coconut oil, melted
1 tbsp peanut butter

For the filling:

3 tbsp maple syrup
2 tbsp melted coconut oil
1 tbsp cacao powder
50g vegan dark chocolate (60% or higher), melted
½ tsp vanilla extract
50ml oat milk
handful of cashews, to decorate

If you crave something sweet, I encourage you to try these. Dark chocolate is a good source of magnesium, which is depleted by stress and inflammation, and levels can drop prior to menstruation. Low magnesium has been linked to symptoms of PMS. Dark chocolate is also a good source of copper and iron and has been shown to support mood through the production of our happy hormones, serotonin and dopamine.

1 Drain the cashew nuts and put them in a food processor along with the oats, dates and coconut oil. Pulse the mixture until it has a dough-like consistency.

2 Line a 20cm square brownie tin or baking tray with baking paper. Pack the crust mixture into the tray, pressing it in very firmly so that it holds together.

3 Clean out the food processor and add all the filling ingredients. Pulse until the mixture is smooth and creamy.

4 Pour the filling over the crust and spread evenly. Sprinkle over the remaining cashews, to decorate.

5 Place in the fridge for 6 hours to harden. Slice into 16 bars and store in an airtight container the fridge for up to 2 weeks.

Gut health

Among the most common ailments I deal with in practice are digestive issues like bloating, constipation and abdominal cramping. Often people are looking for a quick fix, but some of the most meaningful consultations I have with patients involve addressing their diet and nutrition. Many symptoms of irritable bowel syndrome (IBS), for example, can be alleviated by nourishing our microbiome and breaking that state of dysbiosis in the gut. Dysbiosis is a fancy word that means an imbalance in our gut microbes.

My interest and passion for gut health was ignited many years ago when I was 18 and working as a shop assistant in a pharmacy in town. At this point in my life I was living in a chronic state of stress, rushing from one thing to the next and never truly living in the present moment. Due to my diet and lifestyle, which at the time consisted of very little sleep and grabbing whatever processed food I could while on the go, my physical and emotional health were at an all-time low. My skin was constantly breaking out and my mood was low. What I didn't understand at the time was that my diet had such a direct impact on all these factors.

A woman called Lisa, who worked in a colonic irrigation clinic below the pharmacy I worked in kindly offered to sit down with me and go through my diet and lifestyle. It was the first time I had discussed my diet and nutrition with anyone. I told Lisa all the digestive issues I was experiencing – bloating, constipation and abdominal pain – all classic features of IBS with constipation (IBS-C). Instead of reaching for medications I was determined to change my lifestyle to see if I could really cleanse from within. I had seen kombucha, kimchi, kefir and sauerkraut in shops but never really knew what they were, but now I became more and more interested in fermented foods, which are among the most ancient foods we have.

Our 'second brain'

More often than not, people suffering with similar physical digestive symptoms to my own also admit to feeling emotional symptoms like anxiety and depression. For decades we believed that anxiety and depression contributed to bloating, pain, stomach upset, constipation and diarrhoea. In part that is true, but a growing body of research suggests that it may in fact be the other way around. Evidence suggests that irritation in the gastrointestinal system may send signals to the central nervous system (CNS) that trigger mood changes.

Have you ever 'gone with your gut' or felt 'butterflies in your stomach' when you've been nervous? These are signals from our 'second brain', which comprises more than 100 million nerve cells in our digestive tract, also known as the enteric nervous system (ENS). The main role of our ENS is to control digestion, from swallowing and nutrient absorption to elimination. Although the ENS is not capable of forming thoughts it can communicate with

FRUIT	VEGETABLES	GRAINS AND STARCHES	LEGUMES	NUTS AND SEEDS	FRESH HERBS
Apple	Asparagus	Barley	Black beans	Almonds	Basil
Apricot	Broccoli	Brown rice	Black-eyed peas	Brazil nuts	Chives
Avocado	Brussels sprouts	Buckwheat	Butter beans	Chestnuts	Coriander
Banana	Butternut squash	Corn	Cannellini beans	Cashews	Dill
Blueberries	Cabbage	Faro	Chickpeas	Chia seeds	Garlic
Coconut	Carrot	Quinoa	Fava beans	Cumin	Ginger
Cucumber	Cauliflower	Red potato	Haricot beans	Flaxseeds	Mint
Dates	Celery	Sweet potato	Kidney beans	Hazelnuts	Parsley
Figs	Kale	White potato	Lentils	Hemp seeds	Thyme
Grapes	Lettuce	Whole wheat	Pinto beans	Macadamias	
Grapefruit	Okra		Soybeans (edamame, tofu)	Peanuts	
Kiwi	Onion			Pecans	
Lemon	Parsnip			Pine nuts	
Lime	Peas			Pistachios	
Mango	Peppers			Pumpkin seeds	
Olives	Pumpkin			Sunflower seeds	
Orange	Radish			Walnuts	
Papaya	Runner beans				
Peach	Spinach				
Pear	Spring onion				
Plum	Swiss chard				
Pomegranate	Turnips				
Raisins	Watercress				
Raspberries					
Strawberries					
Tomato					
Watermelon					

our brain. The two are connected via the vagus nerve and the communication between the gut and the brain is known as the gut–brain axis. Pretty cool, right? Two of the treatments for IBS that does not respond to diet and lifestyle changes are antidepressants and cognitive behavioural therapy (CBT). This new understanding of the CNS–ENS connection explains the effectiveness of these types of treatment. I found the idea that our two brains 'talk' to each other so profound that it shifted how I looked after my own digestive health. I began to cut down on processed foods and refined sugar and started to include more fruit, vegetables, whole grains and fermented foods in my diet. After a matter of months, not only had my symptoms of 'lazy bowel' disappeared but I was sleeping better, my mood was

	SERVING SIZE	FIBRE (GRAMS)
FRUITS		
Banana	1 medium	3.0
Raspberries	120g	8.0
Apple (with skin)	1 medium	4.5
Orange	1 medium	3.0
Pear	1 medium	5.5
Strawberries	120g	3.0
VEGETABLES		
Artichoke	1 medium	6.0
Broccoli	90g	4.6
Carrot	1 medium	2.0
Cauliflower	100g	3.0
Spinach, boiled	30g	4.4
Green peas	150g	7.0
GRAINS AND STARCHES		
White potato with skin, baked	1 medium	4.0
Sweet potato with skin, baked	1 medium	5.0
Oats	50g	4.5

brighter, and I had more energy. That shift was one of the most beneficial I ever made for my health, both physically and mentally.

Our gut also produces important neurotransmitters. These are chemical messengers our bodies need to function. Serotonin is a neurotransmitter that contributes to feelings of happiness, and a large proportion of serotonin is produced in the gut. Our gut microbes also produce another important neurotransmitter called gamma-aminobutyric acid (GABA), which helps to control feelings of fear, stress and anxiety and is known for its calming effect. Studies in mice have shown that certain probiotics can increase the production of GABA and reduce anxiety. So how can we increase the different types of probiotics in our

guts? Well, the American Gut Project, which is the largest study published to date of the human microbiome, found that people who ate more than 30 plant foods per week had gut microbes that were more diverse than those who ate ten or fewer types of plant food per week. The research also showed that those who hit the 30 mark had more probiotics that produce short-chain fatty acids, which have been shown to reduce the risk of bowel cancer.

Thirty plants a week

We are all familiar with getting our five a day, but less is known about aiming for 30+ plant-based foods a week. This is not a diet trend or fad and I think we need to look further than quick fixes and focus more on sustainable goals that we can implement in our daily lives. The key here is variety; this improves our gut health by encouraging the growth of different species of bacteria. A more diverse microbiome results in a more resilient and stable microbial community that is better armed to protect our overall health.

Eating over 30 plant-based foods per week may sound like a challenge but it is an enjoyable routine to 'spice' up your dishes – literally! Herbs and spices count as plant-based foods, and I've included a template below so you can try incorporating them into some of your meals and ticking them off as you go. Each food group counts only once in the week. I like to add mixed seeds and nuts to salads or porridge as an easy way to increase the number.

Here are a few of my top tips to help get you started.

- **Get the family involved**
  Make a list and keep it on the fridge to track your progress and see who can hit the target … the winner gets the end of week meal cooked for them!
- **Use frozen fruit and vegetables**
  How many of us go out and stock the fridge full of colourful fruit and vegetables only to have them wilt away in a matter of days? To combat this, I always freeze my blueberries (which are a delicious addition to a warm bowl of porridge), for example. Next time you're in the shops have a look at the frozen vegetable section – some of my monthly picks include cauliflower rice, peas, sweetcorn and broccoli.
- **Implement a meat-free Monday**
  I have some delicious vegetarian and vegan options in the vegetarian/vegan health chapter.

Facts on fibre

Fibre is a type of carbohydrate that our body can't break down, so it passes through our gut without being absorbed, but bacteria in our guts ferment it and use it as fuel.

There are two types of fibre:
- **Insoluble fibre** adds bulk to your stool and helps pass food more quickly through the intestines. It also helps balance the pH in your intestine and may prevent diverticulitis (inflammation of the intestine) as well as reducing the development of haemorrhoids and colon cancer. This type of fibre is found on the outer layer of plants, for example potatoes. Good sources are:
  - **Nuts and seeds**
  - **Wholegrain foods**
  - **Green beans**
  - **Cauliflower**

- **Soluble fibre** combines with water to form a gel-like substance with food. This slows down digestion and helps to make you feel full. It also helps lower the risk of heart disease, reduce LDL cholesterol and regulate blood sugar. This type of fibre is found in:
  - **Grains:** oats, barley, bran
  - **Legumes:** beans, peas, lentils
  - **Fruit:** apples, pears, berries
  - **Flaxseeds**
  - **Vegetables:** Brussels sprouts, courgettes

Fibre is essential to our health. Not only does it help to make us feel full, but it also helps to stabilise blood sugar and lower cholesterol. In addition, it promotes a healthier gut. We should aim to be eating roughly 25–30g of fibre each day. I find breakfast an opportune time to load up on fibre-rich foods.

The general rule for increasing your fibre intake is to do so gradually to avoid overloading your gut; increasing your fibre intake too quickly can lead to bloating and gas. And if you don't drink enough water when eating high-fibre foods this can lead to bloating and constipation.

What about supplements?

There are many types of fibre supplements on the market, such as psyllium, inulin and wheat dextrin, and we often recommend them to patients who are experiencing constipation and find it difficult to include fibre in their diet. But food is the best source for your body and your gut bacteria. I would never expect anyone to count the grams of fibre they consume each day, but it is more important to be aware of your intake. Here's a little reference to simplify the complexity of fibre!

Gut-friendly glossary

Probiotics: live 'friendly' bacteria usually found in fermented foods like yoghurt, sauerkraut, kombucha and kefir.

Prebiotics: A type of fibre that helps to feed probiotics, typically found in garlic, onions, oats, bananas, apples and asparagus.

Digestive enzymes: Compounds that help to break down our food so that it can be easily absorbed and used by the body. These are found in papayas, avocados, kefir, mango and pineapple.

Polyphenols: Plant compounds that contain antioxidants and act similarly to prebiotics. Found in foods like avocado, blueberries, dark chocolate and apples.

Flavonoids: A group of polyphenols that are found in plant-based foods. They have beneficial anti-inflammatory effects and help to protect cells from damage that can lead to disease.

Mexican scramble

Gut health

Vegetarian

Fitness

Cognitive health

Serves 2

Prep: 5 minutes

Cook: 10 minutes

Nutrients per serving

500 Calories (kcal) **500**

Carbohydrates (g) **47g**

Protein (g) **28**

Fat (g) **32**

Ingredients

4 eggs
1 red pepper, diced
1 green chilli, deseeded and diced
1 spring onion, chopped
1 tsp ground cumin
1 tbsp olive oil
170g black beans, drained
1 avocado
sourdough bread

This is good for breakfast or lunch, and is quick and easy to make, packed with flavour, and contains 7 of your 30-plants-per-week target! Black beans are a rich source of fibre and avocados are a good source of polyphenols. Cumin (which also counts as a plant-based food) stimulates the production of digestive enzymes, which are needed for the breakdown and absorption of nutrients in the gut.

1 Whisk together the eggs, diced pepper, diced chilli, spring onion and cumin and set aside.

2 Heat the oil in a frying pan, add the black beans and fry for 5 minutes, stirring often.

3 Add the egg mixture to the pan and cook until the eggs are cooked fully and have reached your desired consistency.

4 Slice the avocado and layer over sourdough bread (one of my favourite fermented foods!) before topping with the egg scramble.

Apple pie overnight oats

Gut health   Vegan   Cognitive health   Pregnancy and fertility   Immune health   Heart health

Serves 2

Prep: 15 minutes, plus 6 hours chilling

Cook: 12 minutes

Nutrients per serving

Calories (kcal) **435**

Carbohydrates (g) **53**

Protein (g) **13**

Fat (g) **16**

Ingredients

1 red apple, chopped
2 tbsp maple syrup
1 tsp ground cinnamon
100g porridge oats
300ml unsweetened almond milk
1 tbsp chia seeds
2 tbsp almond butter

Oats and almonds are great sources of prebiotic fibre. Apples contain pectin, a compound that increases butyrate levels (one of our three main short-chain fatty acids). This feeds the friendly bacteria and reduces harmful strains. Chia seeds are a good source of soluble fibre, which helps prevent blood sugar spikes after eating and promotes a feeling of fullness. They are also an excellent source of heart-healthy omega-3 fatty acids.

1 Put the chopped apple, maple syrup and cinnamon in a small saucepan on a low heat and cover. Cook for 10 minutes, stirring occasionally, or until the apple is soft.

2 Remove the lid and turn the heat up to medium, cooking for 2 more minutes, stirring constantly, to evaporate some of the liquid. Turn off the heat and set aside.

3 Mix together the oats, almond milk, chia seeds and almond butter in a small bowl, stirring well.

4 Divide half the apple mixture between two sealable jars or Tupperware containers, pour the oat mixture on top and add the remaining apple mixture on top of the oats. Put in the fridge overnight or for at least 6 hours.

5 Top with a dollop of probiotic-rich yoghurt of choice or seed cycling granola (see page 89) or raisins. Overnight oats will keep in the fridge for 2–3 days.

Oat bran raspberry muffins

Gut health

Vegetarian

Heart health

Pregnancy
and fertility

Hormonal
health

Makes 12 muffins

Prep: 10 minutes

Cook: 20 minutes

Nutrients per serving

Calories (kcal) **215**

Protein (g) **7.5**

Carbohydrates (g) **25**

Fat (g) **13**

Ingredients

100ml vegetable oil
2 tbsp honey
300g natural yoghurt
1 egg
300g oat bran
100g plain white flour
1 tbsp baking powder
2 bananas
1 tsp vanilla extract
100g raspberries

Low in refined sugar and high in fibre, these are great warmed through and served with fruit and yoghurt or grabbed to eat on the go. Oat bran contains a soluble fibre called beta-glucan, which has prebiotic effects, helping to promote the growth of beneficial bacteria in the gut, which can support overall gut health. I often make these over the weekend and take them to work during the week.

1 Preheat the oven to 220°C/200°C fan/gas mark 7 and line a 12-hole muffin tray with paper cases.
2 Put the oil, honey, yoghurt and egg in a large mixing bowl and whisk until well mixed. Add the oat bran, flour and baking powder to the bowl and fold together. Then mash the bananas and add to the mixture, along with the vanilla extract and raspberries.
3 Spoon the mixture into the muffin tin and level off the tops.
4 Bake for 20 minutes until golden and risen.
5 Transfer to a wire rack and allow to cool, then store in an airtight container.

Gut-loving chickpea and cauliflower salad

Gut health

Vegan

Hormonal health

Skin health

Pregnancy and fertility

Serves 2

Prep: 10 minutes

Cook: 30 minutes

Nutrients per serving

Calories (kcal) **510**

Carbohydrates (g) **55**

Protein (g) **16**

Fat (g) **4**

Ingredients

1 medium sweet potato, chopped
½ head of cauliflower, florets
  separated
200g tinned chickpeas
1 clove garlic, unpeeled (for the
  dressing)
1 tsp ground cumin
1 tsp smoked paprika
1 tbsp olive oil
90g couscous
1 vegetable stock cube dissolved in
  1 cup boiled water
50g spinach
10 cherry tomatoes, halved
2 tbsp pumpkin seeds

For the dressing:
200ml coconut yoghurt
1 tsp olive oil
juice of ½ lemon
black pepper, to taste

This is a perfect midweek lunch that is super easy to make and full of flavour. Cauliflower is a good source of both soluble and insoluble fibre, and it also contains several compounds that have anti-inflammatory properties. It is also a good source of inulin, a prebiotic that feeds good bacteria in the gut.

1 Preheat the oven to 220°C/200°C fan/gas mark 7.
2 Put the sweet potato and cauliflower in a roasting dish, drain the chickpeas and add to the dish along with the garlic clove, cumin and paprika. Drizzle the olive oil over and cook in the oven for 30 minutes.
3 Put the couscous in a small bowl, add the vegetable stock and cover (I use a large plate to cover). The couscous should absorb the stock in 10 minutes.
4 To make the dressing, combine all the ingredients in a small bowl or jug. Take the garlic clove out of the roasting dish and squeeze the soft garlic into the dressing. Stir well.
5 Put the couscous, roasted vegetables, spinach and cherry tomatoes in a bowl and mix together. Spoon the dressing over the salad and top with the pumpkin seeds.

Lentil Bolognese

Gut health   Vegetarian   Fitness   Heart health   Skin health   Immune health

Serves 4

Prep: 10 minutes

Cook: 40 minutes

Nutrients per serving

Calories (kcal) **610**

Carbohydrates (g) **90**

Protein (g) **38**

Fat (g) **16**

Ingredients

2 tbsp olive oil

1 onion, diced

150g celery, chopped

200g carrots, diced

3 garlic cloves, finely chopped

1 tsp dried thyme

1 tbsp tomato purée

generous splash of red wine (optional)

400g tinned chopped tomatoes

400g tinned lentils

800ml vegetable stock

2 tsp balsamic vinegar

80g crushed walnuts or pecans

240g wholemeal pasta

Parmesan cheese, fresh basil or chilli flakes, to serve (optional)

This rich and hearty pasta dish has become a staple on my 'meat-free Monday' dinner menu. Lentils are a great source of protein and micronutrients and contain a good amount of prebiotics. This nourishing vegan-friendly meal is one the whole family will enjoy.

1 Heat the oil in a large pan on a medium-high heat, sauté the onion for 5 minutes and lower the heat to medium. Add the celery, carrots, garlic and thyme and sauté for 8 minutes, stirring.

2 Add the tomato purée and deglaze with a splash of red wine (optional). Add the chopped tomatoes and cook for 5 minutes.

3 Drain and rinse the lentils and add them to the pan with the vegetable stock, balsamic vinegar and crushed nuts. Bring to the boil, cover with a lid and lower the heat to low, simmer gently for 15-20 minutes.

4 Cook pasta according to packet instructions, drain and add to the pan, stir well and serve with Parmesan cheese, chilli flakes or fresh basil leaves, if desired.

Coconut chickpea curry

 Gut health

 Vegan

 Immune health

 Skin health

Hormonal health

Serves 4

Prep: 10 mins

Cook: 25 mins

Nutrients per serving

Calories (kcal) **471**

Carbohydrates (g) **65**

Protein (g) **11**

Fat (g) **12**

Ingredients

1 tbsp coconut oil
1 red onion, chopped
1 red pepper, chopped
1 courgette, chopped
1 garlic clove, finely chopped
2 tsp grated ginger
½ tsp turmeric
½ tsp cayenne pepper
250g brown rice
1½ tins light coconut milk
3 tbsp yellow curry paste
250ml vegetable stock
400g tinned chickpeas
juice of ½ lime
120g fresh spinach

This is one of my ultimate weeknight dinners. Growing up, one of my favourite takeaways was some form of curry, and this dish is my go-to when I am craving something comforting. It is so quick and easy to make, and packed full of flavour and bursting with fibre and essential micronutrients. I hope this will become a staple in your kitchen too!

1 In a large pan, heat the coconut oil over a medium heat and add the onion, pepper and courgette. Cook, stirring frequently, until the onion is soft and starting to brown.

2 Reduce the heat and add the garlic and ginger. Cook, stirring for 60 seconds, then add the turmeric and cayenne pepper and cook for 30 seconds more to toast the spices.

3 Cook the brown rice according to instructions on the packet.

4 While the rice is cooking, add the coconut milk, curry paste, vegetable stock and chickpeas to the pan and bring the mixture to the boil. Reduce the heat to medium-low and simmer for 10 minutes or until reduced slightly.

5 Add the lime juice and spinach and stir for two minutes. Serve warm with the rice.

Carrot and miso soup

Gut health   Immune health   Bone health   Cognitive health

Serves 4

Prep: 10 minutes

Cook: 50 minutes

Nutrients per serving

Calories (kcal) **110**

Carbohydrates (g) **17**

Protein (g) **3**

Fat (g) **3**

Ingredients

1 onion, diced
500g carrot, diced
4 cloves garlic, peeled
1 tbsp oil
handful of cashew nuts
1l vegetable stock
3 tbsp white miso paste
salt and pepper to taste

This soup is rich and creamy without using cream – the cashew nuts do the job instead. It also uses gut-friendly miso paste. Miso is a fermented food, which means that it contains live bacteria that can help promote the growth of beneficial bacteria in the gut. The fermentation process also increases the availability of nutrients in the miso, including vitamins B and K, which can further support gut health.

Method

1 Preheat the oven to 200°C/180°C fan/gas mark 6.
2 Put the carrots and garlic in a roasting tin and roast for 25 minutes.
3 Sauté the diced onion in the olive oil in a large saucepan over a medium heat for 10 minutes until browned. Then add the roasted vegetables and cashews and stir for 5 minutes. Add 800ml of the vegetable stock and the miso paste. Cover the saucepan with a lid and simmer for 10 minutes.
4 Blend using a food processor and slowly add the remaining stock until desired consistency is reached.

Miso salmon and sweet potato

 Gut health Bone health Cognitive health Hormonal health Skin health Fitness

Serves 2

Prep: 10 minutes

Cook: 40 minutes

Nutrients per serving

Calories (kcal) **400**

Carbohydrates (g) **37.5**

Protein (g) **36.5**

Fat (g) **31**

Ingredients

2 medium sweet potatoes
2 salmon fillets
100g spinach
1 avocado, sliced
2 tbsp cottage cheese (optional)

For the marinade

1 tbsp white miso
1 tbsp soy sauce
1 clove garlic, minced
1 tbsp honey
thumb-sized piece of ginger,
   finely grated

When I told my friends about this book, one of the first questions was, 'Are you going to include salmon and sweet potato?' While I'm all about trying new things, I also like sticking to what I know! I've taken my habitual Monday night dinner and added some gut-loving ingredients. Miso, made by fermenting beans with koji, a fungal culture, is a great source of probiotics, iron, phosphorus, calcium and B vitamins.

1 Preheat the oven to 210°C/190°C fan/gas mark 6. Line a baking tray with parchment paper, prick the sweet potatoes all over with a fork and place them on the tray. Bake for 25 minutes.

2 Meanwhile, prepare the marinade by whisking together all the ingredients with 100ml of water. Put the salmon on a piece of tinfoil large enough to wrap around them, drizzle half the marinade over the fish and fold the tinfoil over two fillets.

3 After 25 minutes, turn the sweet potatoes, put the salmon fillets in the oven and cook for a further 15 minutes.

4 Remove the sweet potatoes and salmon from the oven, drizzle the reserved marinade over the salmon and serve warm on a bed of spinach and sliced avocado.

5 Add 1 tbsp of cottage cheese to each sweet potato to increase protein intake, if desired.

Greek yoghurt chocolate mousse

Gut health   Pregnancy and fertility   Cognitive health   Bone health   Vegetarian

Serves 4

Prep: 30 minutes, plus four hours chilling

Cook: 5 minutes

Nutrients per serving

Calories (kcal) **308**

Carbohydrates (g) **30.5**

Protein (g) **5**

Fat (g) **16**

Ingredients

180g dark chocolate
120ml unsweetened almond milk
1 tsp vanilla extract
1 tbsp maple syrup
500g Greek yoghurt
handful of strawberries and
    chopped dark chocolate, to serve

Once, on holiday, Dad and I ordered seconds of chocolate mousse and when the waiter came to take our dishes, we ordered thirds. He said, 'Really? Are you sure?' and we burst out laughing. Food can bring back so many memories. The Greek yoghurt in this recipe nourishes the gut with live probiotic strains, and the prebiotic properties of dark chocolate and its anti-inflammatory polyphenols makes this one of my favourite gut-loving snacks.

1 Heat the chocolate and almond milk together over a low heat in a small saucepan until the chocolate has melted.
2 Remove from heat and whisk in the vanilla extract and maple syrup. Allow the mixture to cool for 20 minutes before whisking in the Greek yoghurt until smooth.
3 Divide the mixture into four ramekins and pop into the fridge for four hours to set, then garnish with fresh strawberries.

Heart health

The circulatory system, also called the cardiovascular system, is made up of the heart and blood vessels. One of its functions is to deliver oxygen around the body. Blood is pumped from our heart to our lungs, where it collects oxygen. The heart then sends this oxygenated blood throughout the body to be used by muscles, organs, tissues and cells. Arteries carry oxygenated blood to the rest of the body and veins carry oxygen-poor blood back to the heart to start the circulation process again.

Another function of the circulatory system is to remove waste from organs and cells. This waste includes carbon dioxide from respiration (breathing), chemical by-products from organs and toxins from what we eat and drink.

Cardiovascular diseases

A report carried out by researchers at Trinity College Dublin highlighted the main cause of death in Ireland and found that cancer contributed to 31 per cent of deaths in 2018 while diseases of the circulatory system accounted for 29 per cent. This is a staggering statistic. It is clear that cardiovascular disease (CVD) is a leading cause of death, despite nearly 80 per cent of premature CVD being

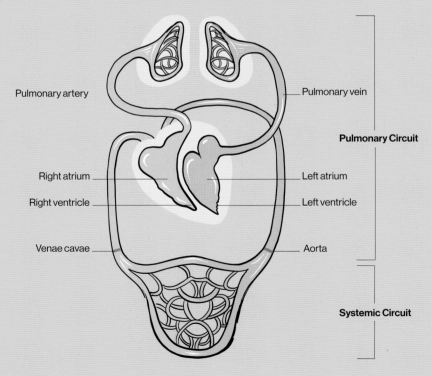

Pulmonary artery

Pulmonary vein

Pulmonary Circuit

Right atrium

Left atrium

Right ventricle

Left ventricle

Venae cavae

Aorta

Systemic Circuit

preventable. Diet and lifestyle can play a huge role in preventing circulatory diseases, and since prevention is better than a cure, we really need to be proactive about our health in order to change this statistic.

Let's take a closer look at what can go wrong in our circulatory system, and the factors that can negatively impact or improve our circulatory health.

There are a number of types of heart disease that fall under the umbrella term of 'cardiovascular disease'. The good news is that so many risk factors are modifiable, meaning that we can actively decrease our individual risk of developing cardiovascular diseases. This chapter will highlight how we can do that.

Atherosclerosis

Atherosclerosis occurs when fatty deposits build up within the arteries, which causes them to narrow, making it more difficult for blood to flow through them. This increases your risk for heart attack and stroke.

It can occur with no symptoms at all or you may experience chest pain, pain in the arms and legs (especially during exercise), shortness of breath, fatigue and feeling weak and confused. Risk factors include:

- **Smoking**
- **High cholesterol**
- **High blood pressure**
- **Having relatives who have cardiovascular disease**
- **Being over 65 years of age.**

Coronary artery disease (CAD)

CAD is caused by atherosclerosis in the coronary arteries, the arteries that carry blood to the heart. This puts you at higher risk of suffering a heart attack. CAD is the most common cause of heart attacks and can also lead to heart failure.

Congestive heart failure

This is a long-term serious health condition that gets worse over time. The function of the heart gradually declines. This makes the heart start pumping faster and it may also get bigger. You will start to feel fatigued and can develop problems with breathing.

Heart valve disease

The heart has four valves that keep blood moving in the right direction. As the heart muscle beats, the valves open and close. Heart valve disease happens when one or more of the valves no longer work they way they used to. Some of the things that can cause heart valve disease are:

- **Stenosis:** The flaps of the heart valves become too thick or stiff, making it harder for blood to flow through.
- **Regurgitation:** The flaps of the valve do not close properly. This causes blood to leak backwards into the heart.
- **Atresia:** Instead of the valves opening and closing, a solid piece of tissue blocks blood flow

Cardiomyopathy

There are two types of cardiomyopathy: dilated and hypertrophic. Cardiomyopathy is a disease of the heart muscle and the condition makes it harder for the heart to pump blood throughout the body. It can eventually lead to heart failure.

Again, this condition can be symptomless so you may not even know you have it, but as the disease progresses symptoms can include:

- **Breathlessness with activity or at rest**
- **Swollen legs, ankles and feet**
- **Fatigue**
- **Coughing when lying down**
- **Rapid, pounding or fluttering heartbeats**

Often the cause is unknown but it can be an inherited condition and risk factors for acquired cardiomyopathy include:

- **Long-term high blood pressure**
- **Heart valve problems**
- **Covid-19**
- **Metabolic disorders like obesity or diabetes**
- **Lack of essential vitamins like thiamine (B1)**
- **Iron build-up in the heart muscle (hemochromatosis)**
- **Chronic alcohol abuse**

Arrhythmia

This condition has to do with the way the heart beats. In a normal healthy person the heart will slow at rest and speed up with activity. In cases of arrhythmia, there are unusual heartbeats. If left untreated it can result in heart attack and/or stroke.

Some people with heart disease have no symptoms at all until they have a heart attack. That is why it's important to get screened if you believe you may be at risk of developing heart disease.

Risk factors include:

- **High blood pressure**
- **High blood cholesterol levels**
- **Family history of heart problems**
- **Obesity**
- **Diabetes**
- **Smoking**
- **Increasing age**
- **Sedentary lifestyle/not enough exercise.**

What is cholesterol?

Cholesterol is a fatty substance found in blood and produced by the liver or obtained through the foods we eat. Our bodies need a certain amount of cholesterol to produce hormones, to help digestion and for normal cell function, so not all cholesterol is bad.

There are two types of cholesterol:

- **HDL (high-density lipoprotein):** Also known as 'good' cholesterol because it can transport 'bad' cholesterol away from the arteries and to the liver to be broken down and removed from the body. HDL cholesterol is associated with a decreased risk of coronary artery disease.
- **LDL (low-density lipoprotein):** Known as 'bad' cholesterol because it can stick to the walls of the arteries, causing them to narrow. If the arteries that carry blood to the heart get clogged and blocked it can lead to a heart attack. Or if the arteries that carry blood to your brain get clogged this can lead to a stroke.
- **Triglycerides** are another type of fat found in blood. They can also contribute to the narrowing of arteries, increasing your risk for heart disease. Levels are affected by what we eat; high-sugar and highly processed foods can increase triglyceride levels.

Factors that increase cholesterol include: not being active enough; smoking; obesity; an unhealthy diet; and non-modifiable factors like gender, age, family history and ethnicity.

The Mediterranean diet

A cardioprotective Mediterranean diet is the first-line dietary approach for preventing heart disease and stroke. Studies have shown that people who consume a Mediterranean diet are less likely to have diabetes, high blood pressure and raised cholesterol, all of which are risk factors for heart disease. The Mediterranean diet includes:

- **Fruit and vegetables**
- **Whole grains**
- **Beans, nuts, seeds, legumes**
- **Olive oils**
- **Fish**

- **Good fats (avocado, salmon, walnuts, sesame oil)**
- **Moderate wine consumption**
- **Lower consumption of processed foods, dairy products, red meat and vegetable oils**

The Mediterranean diet pattern consists of nutrients from:
- **Monounsaturated fatty acids, PUFAs**
- **Antioxidants (sulphur compounds, beta-carotene, anthocyanins and other flavonoids)**
- **Fat-soluble vitamins like A, D and E**
- **Minerals (magnesium, calcium, iodine, zinc and selenium)**

In general, red meats (beef, lamb and pork) tend to be higher in saturated fat than fish, plant proteins and skinless chicken. Saturated fats can raise your blood cholesterol levels and increase heart disease risk. Everything in moderation and if choosing poultry, beef or other meats try to pick lean meat, skinless poultry and unprocessed forms of meat.

The dietary approach to stop hypertension (DASH) diet

Originating in America in the 1990s, the DASH diet was designed to help treat or prevent high blood pressure. The DASH diet includes:
- **Fruit and vegetables**
- **Wholegrains**
- **Fish**
- **Low-fat dairy products**
- **Poultry, beans, nuts**
- **Foods rich in potassium, calcium and magnesium (regulates blood pressure)**
- **Low in sodium, alcohol, saturated fat, sugar**

Both the Mediterranean and the DASH diet are flexible and balanced eating plans. The Mediterranean diet focuses on promoting general cardiovascular health, whereas the DASH diet is mainly concerned with lowering blood pressure.

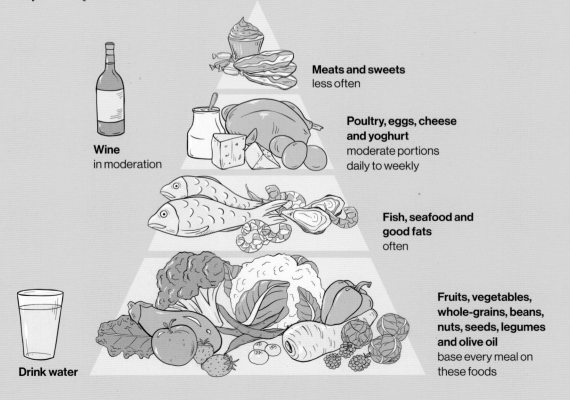

Meats and sweets
less often

Poultry, eggs, cheese and yoghurt
moderate portions
daily to weekly

Fish, seafood and good fats
often

Fruits, vegetables, whole-grains, beans, nuts, seeds, legumes and olive oil
base every meal on these foods

Wine
in moderation

Drink water

Heart-healthy nutrition

Your heart-healthy nutrition should come from some of the following foods:

- **Whole grains**: oats, wholegrain bread, brown rice
- **Fruit**: apples, bananas, pears, prunes, grapes, oranges
- **Vegetables**: leafy greens (kale, spinach, cabbage), carrots, beetroot, broccoli
- **Protein-rich foods:**
  - Fish high in omega-3 fatty acids (salmon, tuna, trout)
  - Eggs
  - Lean meats (95 per cent lean minced beef, pork tenderloin, skinless turkey or chicken)
  - Nuts and seeds
  - Soy products (tofu, tempeh)
  - Legumes (chickpeas, kidney beans, lentils, butter beans, cannellini beans)

- **Oils and foods rich in monounsaturated and polyunsaturated fats:**
  - Olive, sesame, sunflower and soybean oils
  - Walnuts, almonds, pine nuts
  - Sesame, sunflower, pumpkin and flaxseeds
  - Avocados
  - Salmon and trout

What about eggs?

Eggs are a rich source of protein and vitamins. One large egg contains roughly six grams of protein. They are one of the few food sources of vitamin D (to support bone and immune health), and they contain choline (to aid metabolism and liver function).

Egg yolks may be beneficial for eye health as they contain lutein and zeaxanthin, which studies have shown reduce the risk of macular degeneration and cataracts. However, the

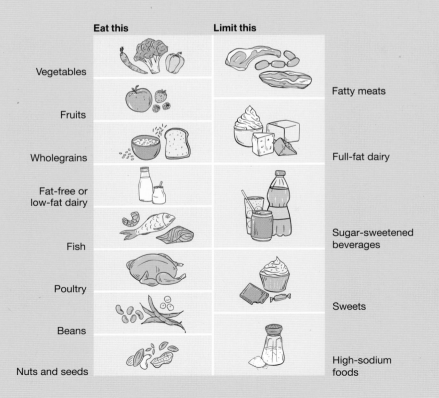

Eat this | Limit this

Vegetables

Fruits

Wholegrains

Fat-free or low-fat dairy

Fish

Poultry

Beans

Nuts and seeds

Fatty meats

Full-fat dairy

Sugar-sweetened beverages

Sweets

High-sodium foods

yolk is also a source of cholesterol. One large egg contains around 186mg of cholesterol. For years it was recommended to limit egg consumption in order to lower cholesterol, but studies have found that those with higher cholesterol were also eating their eggs with foods high in trans fats like sausages and rashers. The way eggs are cooked also plays a role in the risk of developing heart disease. Frying eggs in butter or oil puts you at a greater risk than poaching or baking them.

More recent research has suggested that eating up to 7 eggs per week will not increase your risk of developing heart disease. One study looked at half a million people in China over 9 years and found eating one egg per day did not increase heart disease risk.

But you have to look at the bigger picture and assess your own individual risk factors. If you have diabetes or consume a large amount of red meat you will be at a higher risk of developing heart disease versus a vegetarian with no chronic health conditions. Since we should aim to keep our daily cholesterol consumption under 300mg per day, if your diet contains minimal other sources of cholesterol an egg a day seems to be okay!

Tip: You can always use egg whites for things like omelettes or scrambled eggs and discard the cholesterol-rich yolk if desired.

Foods to avoid

There are several foods to avoid or limit in order to improve the overall function of the heart.

Sodium
The Food Safety Authority of Ireland recommends that adults consume no more than 4g of sodium per day (1 tsp of table salt contains roughly 2.3g).

Sodium is an essential nutrient needed for plasma volume, normal cell function and transmission of nerve impulses, but excess sodium is linked to adverse health outcomes like high blood pressure. Eating too much salt can raise blood pressure at any age.

Ways to reduce salt intake:
- **Read food labels and choose foods that have less sodium for the same serving size and choose low-sodium or reduced-sodium products.**
- **Choose frozen or fresh foods instead of pre-seasoned, brined, sauce-marinated or processed meats, poultry and vegetables.**
- **Flavour foods with herbs and spices instead of salt.**
- **When cooking at home try to cook from scratch instead of using ready-made sauces and mixes.**

Saturated fats
Most saturated fats come from animal products like cheese, butter and fatty meats. They should account for less than 10 per cent of your total daily calories. Unsaturated fats are found in nuts and vegetable oils.

Added sugars
Limiting your daily intake of calories from sugar each day has many positive effects on your overall health as well as for your cardiovascular health. Your sugar intake should come from natural sources like fruit. Added sugars include corn syrup, dextrose, fructose, glucose, raw sugar and sucrose.
- **Limit sweetened drinks like soft drinks and energy drinks and try not to add sugar to coffee or tea**

Alcohol

Alcohol contains 'empty calories' and provides the body with no nutritional benefit. Alcohol can also raise your blood pressure and levels of triglycerides in your blood. It can also contribute or worsen heart failure in patients who have cardiomyopathy.

If you do drink, spread your alcohol intake over the week and make sure to have alcohol-free days. Aim to drink less than the recommended upper limits: 17 standard drinks a week for men and 11 for women

- **1 pint = 2 standard drinks**
- **1 small glass of wine (100ml) = 1 standard drink**
- **1 spirit (single measure) = 1 standard drink**
- **1 bottle of wine = 7 standard drinks**

Getting moving

Being overweight means that your heart has to work extra hard to pump blood around your body. This extra pressure can cause wear and tear on your heart and blood vessels.

Being physically active burns calories, tones muscles, releases 'happy' hormones and decreases your risk of chronic health conditions like diabetes, heart disease and obesity.

Knowledge is power

Making even the smallest changes can have a profound impact on your overall health. Start small and with consistency you can change your eating and exercise habits.

Cherry tomato egg-white muffins

 Heart health   Cognitive health   Fitness   Vegetarian

Serves 2

Prep: 10 minutes

Cook: 20 minutes

Nutrients per serving

Calories (kcal) **205**

Carbohydrates (g) **5**

Protein (g) **13.5**

Fat (g) **7**

Ingredients

4 large egg whites
½ tsp garlic powder
½ tsp black pepper
2 tbsp pesto
1 spring onion, diced
handful of cherry tomatoes, sliced,
   plus extra to serve (optional)
pea shoots, to serve (optional)

If you have high cholesterol you may want to limit the amount of egg yolk you consume, but you don't have to sacrifice flavour. These egg-white muffins are golden, fluffy and bursting with flavour. You can make them ahead and store them in the fridge; they can be quickly reheated in the microwave or even eaten cold.

1 Preheat the oven to 200°C/180°C fan/gas mark 6. Grease two large ramekins and line them with baking paper.

2 In a large bowl whisk together the egg whites until light and frothy. Add the garlic powder, black pepper and pesto and whisk to combine.

3 Mix in the spring onion and sliced cherry tomatoes and divide the mixture evenly between the ramekins (they should be about ¾ full).

4 Place in the oven and bake until risen, around 20 minutes. Serve with a few tomato slices and some pea shoots, if desired.

Almond butter and date oat pots

Heart health

Bone health

Cognitive health

Gut health

Vegetarian

Serves 2

Prep: 5 minutes

Nutrients per serving

Calories (kcal) **300**

Carbohydrates (g) **34**

Protein (g) **12**

Fat (g) **11**

Ingredients

60g rolled oats
2 tbsp almond butter
2 Medjool dates, chopped
1 tsp vanilla extract
200g Greek yoghurt
1 tsp ground cinnamon
1 tbsp goji berries

Try out these make-ahead overnight oats for a delicious and healthy start to your day. You can use whatever nut butter you like and top with frozen or fresh fruit. Almond butter is high in monounsaturated fats, which can help to reduce LDL (bad) cholesterol levels. Oats and almond butter combined offer a decent serving of fibre, which can help improve heart health by reducing cholesterol levels.

1 Put the oats in a large bowl and add 200ml of boiling water. Add the almond butter, chopped dates and vanilla and stir well. Allow to cool and then mix in the yoghurt. Add in extra water or some unsweetened almond milk if you prefer a looser consistency.

2 Divide the mixture into two sealable containers and sprinkle each with half the cinnamon and goji berries.

3 Store in the fridge for 2-3 days.

Tofu Buddha bowl with coconut peanut sauce

Heart health

Bone health

Pregnancy and fertility

Skin health

Vegetarian

Serves 2

Prep: 30 minutes

Cook: 10 minutes

Nutrients per serving

Calories (kcal) **460**

Carbohydrates (g) **52**

Protein (g) **26**

Fat (g) **16.5**

Ingredients

250g firm tofu
2 tbsp white miso
1 tbsp apple cider vinegar
60g quinoa
1 tbsp olive oil
100g mango, chopped
50g cucumber, chopped
50g sweetcorn
50g black beans, drained and rinsed
1 avocado, sliced
handful of roasted peanuts, to serve (optional)

For the sauce:

80ml coconut milk
2 tbsp creamy peanut butter

Buddha bowls were a staple dish in Australia and since they're hard to find in Ireland I experiment with my own. This dish is packed with antioxidant-rich plants and plant protein from the tofu. The essentials for a Buddha bowl are grains (brown rice, quinoa, barley, bulgur, couscous), vegetables, protein, healthy fat and dressing. You could sprinkle on some nuts, flaxseed or cranberries for some added diversity! These are great to make ahead and store in the fridge.

1 Remove the tofu from the pack, press it to remove excess fluid and chop into bite-size cubes. Add the miso and vinegar to a bowl and whisk to combine. Add the tofu cubes to the miso marinade and stir everything together so that the tofu is coated. Allow to marinate for 30 minutes.

2 While the tofu is marinating, cook the quinoa according to the instructions on the packet.

3 Heat the olive oil in a frying pan over a medium heat and add the tofu cubes. Lightly brown the tofu cubes on all sides. Remove from the heat and allow to cool.

4 To make the sauce, put the coconut milk and peanut butter in a saucepan over a low heat and heat gently for 2–3 minutes, or until combined.

5 Put the quinoa, mango, cucumber, sweetcorn, black beans and sliced avocado in two bowls. Top with the tofu cubes and drizzle with the sauce. Sprinkle over a handful of roasted peanuts to serve, if desired.

Spinach and pesto pasta

Heart health   Gut health   Vegetarian

Serves 4

Prep: 10 minutes

Cook: 20 minutes

Nutrients per serving

Calories (kcal) **395**

Carbohydrates (g) **60**

Protein (g) **24**

Fat (g) **6.5**

Ingredients

1 tbsp olive oil

1 red onion, chopped

100g cherry tomatoes

2 garlic cloves, minced

200g spinach

300g wholewheat spaghetti

4 tbsp cottage cheese

4 tbsp pesto (see the Parmesan-
free version at the end of this
chapter)

½ tsp chilli flakes (optional)

handful of fresh basil, to serve
(optional)

This is a great recipe to fill the family in a hurry! Cottage cheese is lower in saturated fat than hard cheese and is packed with B vitamins and magnesium. Spinach is a good source of antioxidants, including vitamin C and E and beta-carotene, which can help to protect the heart by reducing inflammation and oxidative stress, and potassium, a mineral that can help regulate blood pressure.

1 Heat the olive oil in a frying pan over a medium heat and fry the onion and tomatoes for 10 minutes until softened. Add the garlic and fry for 2 minutes. Add the spinach and 100ml of water, cover and cook for 5 minutes or until the spinach has wilted.

2 Meanwhile, cook the pasta according to the instructions on the packet. Drain and add to the sauce mixture. Add the cottage cheese, pesto and chilli flakes and stir through before plating. Scatter over some fresh basil leaves to serve, if desired.

Fish tacos with tomato salsa

Heart health

Serves 4

Prep: 10 minutes

Cook: 20 minutes

Nutrients per serving

Calories (kcal) **450**

Carbohydrates (g) **27.5**

Protein (g) **33**

Fat (g) **24**

Ingredients

4 tsp smoked paprika
1 tsp ground cumin
2 tsp garlic powder
500g white fish fillets (cod, hake or
   haddock work well)

For the creamy salsa:

4 tbsp cottage cheese
220g cherry tomatoes, halved
1 red onion, diced
1 garlic clove, minced
2 tbsp lime juice
1 tsp black pepper

To serve:

4 wholemeal flour tortillas
1 little gem lettuce, shredded
2 avocados, sliced
shredded lettuce
fresh coriander

Stuck for an idea on what to cook for an easy and tasty midweek dinner? This recipe has you covered! Often fish taco dishes can be laced with trans fats from deep fat frying but this is a lighter, healthier recipe using baked fish that doesn't skimp on flavour, thanks to the spices used to coat the fish.

1 Preheat the oven to 200°C/180°C fan/gas mark 6. In a small bowl combine the paprika, cumin and garlic powder and coat each fish fillet with the seasoning. Lay the fillets on a lined baking tray and bake in the oven for 12–14 minutes or until the fish flakes easily with a fork.
2 While the fish is baking, combine all the salsa ingredients in a bowl and mix together until combined.
3 Warm the tortillas in the oven for about 5 minutes.
4 Flake the fish into bite-sized pieces and divide evenly between the tortillas. Serve with salsa, lettuce, coriander and sliced avocado.

Tuna and sweetcorn baked potato

Heart health

Cognitive health

Fitness

Serves 4

Prep: 10 minutes

Cook: 60 minutes

Nutrients per serving

Calories (kcal) **410**

Carbohydrates (g) **55**

Protein (g) **31.5**

Fat (g) **6.5**

Ingredients

4 large potatoes
400g tinned tuna, drained
400g sweetcorn
4 tbsp low-fat mayonnaise
4 tbsp fat-free natural yoghurt
1 tsp chives
1 red bell pepper, diced
black pepper

One of the easiest lunches to make and great for batch cooking and storing in the fridge – the potatoes can be heated through in the oven or microwave the next day. Potatoes are a great source of fibre and are high in potassium, which helps to manage blood pressure. A comforting and easy lunch option.

1 Preheat the oven to 200°C/180°C fan/gas mark 6. Using a fork, prick the potatoes all over and put on a baking tray. Place in the centre of the oven and cook for an hour, or until the skin is crisp.
2 While the potatoes are cooking, put the tuna, sweetcorn, mayonnaise, yoghurt, chives and diced pepper in a bowl and stir to combine.
3 Remove the potatoes from the oven and allow to cool for 5–10 minutes before slicing through the middle. Add the tuna mixture and a pinch of black pepper if desired.

Fakeaway KFC burger

Heart health

Serves 2

Prep: 10 minutes

Cook: 10 minutes

Nutrients per serving

Calories (kcal) **550**

Carbohydrates (g) **50**

Protein (g) **44**

Fat (g) **16**

Ingredients

2 slices wholemeal bread
1 tsp black pepper
1 tsp dried oregano
1 tsp dried basil
1 tsp garlic powder
2 tsp smoked paprika
1 egg
2 skinless chicken breasts

For the mayonnaise:
2 tbsp low-fat mayonnaise
1 tbsp sundried tomatoes,
    chopped
1 garlic clove, minced
squeeze of lemon juice

To serve:
2 wholemeal pitta pockets
lettuce

Swap your next trip to KFC with this super easy crispy chicken burger recipe. Impress your partner on your next date night at home. Go nude and serve with just lettuce, or pop into wholemeal pitta pockets and finish with a dollop of low-fat garlic mayo. It is also lower in trans fats than your regular takeaway burger!

1 Heat the grill to high. Place the bread slices in a food processor with the black pepper and blitz until breadcrumbs are formed.
2 In a small bowl combine the oregano, basil, garlic powder, paprika and egg and whisk together. Coat each chicken fillet in the mixture then press the chicken into the breadcrumb mix and lay on a lined baking tray.
3 Grill the chicken for about 10 minutes, turning once, until cooked through and golden and crisp on both sides.
4 While the chicken is cooking, combine all the mayonnaise ingredients in a small bowl and set aside.
5 Serve the chicken with lettuce or pitta pockets (or both) and top with mayonnaise.

Hoisin duck noodles

Heart health

Serves 2

Prep: 5 minutes

Cook: 15 minutes

Nutrients per serving

Calories (kcal) **490**

Carbohydrates (g) **53**

Protein (g) **39**

Fat (g) **12**

Ingredients

1 tbsp olive oil

2 skinless duck breast fillets, sliced

6 spring onions, sliced

2 cloves garlic, sliced

1 courgette, sliced

2 tbsp low-salt soy sauce

2 nests wholewheat noodles

4 tbsp hoisin sauce

1 cucumber, spiralised or sliced
   into thin ribbons with a vegetable
   peeler

sesame seeds (optional)

It's nice to switch up your protein sources and I find duck an under-rated member of the poultry family! A nice change from chicken or turkey, these duck noodles are so easy to make and full of flavour. Duck is also a source of heart-healthy omega-3 fatty acids and it contains the amino acid taurine, which is essential for heart function.

1 Put the olive oil in a wok or large frying pan over a medium heat and add the duck. Allow the duck to sizzle for 5–6 minutes, then add the spring onions, garlic, courgette and soy sauce, along with 2–3 tbsp water and stir-fry for 5 minutes.
2 Cook the noodles according to the instructions on the packet. Take the wok off the heat, drain the noodles and add them to the wok. Then add the hoisin sauce and mix through.
3 Divide between two plates and top with the cucumber and sesame seeds, if desired.

Apple and blackberry oat crumble

Heart health   Vegetarian

Serves: 8

Prep:15 minutes

Cook: 40 minutes

Nutrients per serving

Calories (kcal) **185**

Carbohydrates (g) **44**

Protein (g) **3**

Fat (g) **4**

Ingredients

For the filling:
cooking spray oil
7 cooking apples, peeled and
    chopped
100g blackberries
1 tbsp orange zest, grated
2 tbsp maple syrup

For the crumble:
70g porridge oats
120g plain flour
1 tsp ground cinnamon
3 tbsp maple syrup
75g Benecol spread

Apple crumble reminds me of home. Mum often made it after Sunday lunch and it was Dad's favourite, so now every time I have it for dessert I smile and think of him. I think food can evoke many good memories and I hope you enjoy this healthy spin on apple crumble too! This recipe uses Benecol spread instead of butter. It contains a plant sterol ester that has been shown to lower cholesterol, so it is a healthier alternative to butter.

1 Preheat the oven to 200°C/180°C fan/gas mark 6. Spray a baking dish with cooking spray oil and set aside.
2 Put the chopped apples in a bowl with the blackberries, orange zest and maple syrup. Mix together and spoon into the baking dish.
3 To prepare the crumble, combine the oats and flour in a bowl and add the cinnamon and maple syrup. Mix together with a spoon.
4 Add the Benecol and with your fingertips rub the spread into the flour and oat mixture to form a crumbly mixture.
5 Sprinkle the topping over the fruit and bake for 35–40 minutes or until golden.

Parmesan-free pesto

Heart health

Vegan

Makes about 16 tbsp

Prep: 10 minutes

Nutrients per serving (1 tbsp)

Calories (kcal) **45**

Carbohydrates (g) **1.5**

Protein (g) **0.8**

Fat (g) **3.8**

Ingredients

40g fresh basil (large stems removed)

4 tbsp pine nuts

4 garlic cloves, peeled

4 tbsp nutritional yeast

2 tbsp olive oil

4 tbsp water

2 tbsp lemon juice

A cheesy pesto recipe without the cheese! It uses nutritional yeast flakes, which have a delicious nutty and cheesy flavour. They are also an excellent source of vitamin B12 and lower in saturated fats than Parmesan. This recipe is so easy to make. I hope you love it as much as I do!

1. Put the basil, pine nuts, garlic and nutritional yeast in a food processor or blender and blend at high speed until you have a loose mixture.
2. Add 1 tbsp of olive oil and blend, then add another tbsp of oil and blend again. Add the lemon juice and then add the water 1 tbsp at a time until the pesto has reached your desired consistency.
3. Store in a sealed container in the fridge for up to one week.

Bone health

Bone health is important at every stage and age of life. Bones give our bodies support, they allow us to use our muscles to walk and exercise, they protect our organs and store and release calcium.

The human skeleton comprises 206 bones. Each bone is made up of connective tissue reinforced with calcium and specialised bone cells. Blood cells are made within the bone marrow. Our bodies are constantly building up and breaking down bone tissue as needed. In order to maintain healthy bones, we need to eat a balanced and varied diet, engage in regular weight-bearing exercise and produce adequate levels of hormones.

Many people reach their peak bone and muscle mass between the ages of 25 and 30. We begin to lose bone mass as we enter our 40s but we can take steps in order to strengthen our bones.

Bone cells

It is estimated that roughly every decade each bone is rebuilt from scratch; this is because our body is constantly remodelling our skeleton.

Bone marrow is where different types of blood cells are made. Bone marrow makes:

- **White blood cells to support the body's immune system**
- **Red blood cells, which carry oxygen around the body**
- **Platelets, used for blood clotting.**

Lifestyle factors

Our maximum bone strength and size is known as peak bone mass. Although it is largely determined by genetic factors, lifestyle factors such as diet and exercise can have an influence on bone mass potential. Peak bone mass is usually reached between the ages of 25 and 30. The best time to build bone density is during the years of rapid growth. Childhood, adolescence and early adulthood are times where we can increase our bone mass through diet and exercise and by limiting factors that contribute to bone loss such as smoking, inactivity, excessive alcohol and poor nutrition. For the majority of us, bone loss can be slowed by taking steps to ensure we maintain proper nutrition and regular exercise.

It is inevitable that we will all lose bone as we age, but people who have developed higher peak bone mass when they were younger are better protected against osteoporosis and related fractures in later life.

Osteoporosis

Osteoporosis is a bone disease that occurs when bone mineral density and bone mass decreases. This can lead to a decrease in bone strength, which can increase the risk of fractures. It is often referred to as a 'silent' disease as typically there are few, if any, symptoms. Osteoporosis is the main cause of fractures in postmenopausal women and older men. These fractures can occur in any bone but most commonly affect the hip, wrist and vertebrae.

Gender

Women have lower peak bone mass than men. As women have smaller bones with a thinner cortex and smaller diameter, they are more likely than men to develop osteoporosis. Men are still at risk of developing osteoporosis, but at a later stage in life, usually over the age of 70 when bone loss and fracture risk increase.

Vitamin D

Vitamin D plays a role in the body's ability to absorb calcium and that is why it is often contained in calcium supplements.

Some people will require different doses of vitamin D depending on other factors such as co-morbidities, skin type and weight. These are the HSE's guidelines for the average healthy person:

- **0–12 months:** 5 micrograms of D3 every day if they are breast-fed or taking less than 300ml of infant formula per day
- **1–4 years:** 5 micrograms from October to March
- **Adults and children over 4 years:** 10 micrograms or 400 IU
- **Healthy older adults living independently and who get sunlight exposure during summer:** a daily vitamin D supplement of 10 micrograms or 400 IU during the autumn and winter months (October–March)
- **Housebound older adults with minimal sunlight exposure:** a daily vitamin D supplement of 15 micrograms or 600 IU throughout the year

The role of calcium

Calcium is a mineral that our bodies use to build and maintain strong bones and teeth. It is also vital for proper cell functioning, it regulates muscle contractions, including the heartbeat, and it plays a role in blood clotting. It is the building block of bone and a diet rich in calcium is essential to avoid the risk of osteoporosis and associated fractures in later life.

Our skeleton stores around 99 per cent of our body's calcium. If we do not obtain enough calcium through our diet, calcium will be removed from where it is stored in the bones and over time this causes bones to grow weaker.

Adults aged 19–64 need around 700–1,000mg of calcium per day and we should be able to obtain that from our diet. Taking too much calcium (>1,500mg a day) can lead to diarrhoea and stomach pain. Pregnant and lactating women have increased calcium demands and should aim for 1,200mg per day.

Sources of calcium include:
- **Milk, cheese, yoghurt and other dairy sources:**
  - **240ml milk or yoghurt – around 300mg**
  - **30g Cheddar cheese – 200mg**
- **Legumes:**
  - **200g cooked chickpeas – 100mg**
  - **200g cooked white beans – 130mg**
- **Vegetables, including green leafy vegetables like kale, spinach and okra:**
  - **120g raw broccoli –112mg**
  - **120g raw carrots – 36mg**
- **Soy drinks with added calcium**
- **Fish, including fish of which you eat the bones, such as pilchards and sardines:**
  - **120g tinned tuna – 34mg**
  - **60g tinned sardines in oil – 240mg**
- **Fruits:**
  - **150g orange – 60mg**
  - **60g dried figs – 100mg**
- **Nuts and seeds:**
  - **30g almonds – 75mg**
  - **30g tahini paste – 42mg**
  - **30g hazelnuts – 56mg**

- **Other:**
  - 120g tofu → 126mg
  - 100g seaweed → 70mg
  - 100g wakame → 150mg

Calcium through the years

Birth–9 years
Calcium is an essential mineral for babies and children as it is required to grow bones and teeth. Our body needs vitamin D to absorb calcium, so getting enough vitamin D goes hand in hand with getting enough calcium.

Around 200mg of calcium per day is required for the first six months and this increases to roughly 260mg from 7 to 12 months. During this first year both bottle- and breast-fed babies will get enough calcium through milk.

Calcium requirements increase as a child grows, and children aged 1–3 years should be aiming for around 700mg of calcium per day. This equates to one glass of milk, 20g Cheddar cheese and 300g Greek yoghurt.

At 4–8 years calcium requirements increase again to around 1,000mg per day, or the equivalent of about two bowls of yoghurt and one glass of milk.

Puberty: 10–20 years
Puberty is an important time in the development of the skeleton and peak bone mass. Half of total body calcium stores in women and up to two-thirds of calcium stores in men are made during puberty. By the time puberty ends, men tend to have around 50 per cent more body calcium than women.

For girls, having a regular period is a good indicator of health. It is particularly important for bone health as it is a sign that sufficient oestrogen is being produced. Oestrogen is a hormone that can improve calcium absorption in the kidneys and intestines.

Weight-bearing exercise during teenage years is essential for building bone strength. This includes walking and running as well as sports like football and basketball.

Girls who exercise excessively can lose too much weight which can cause hormonal changes leading to a loss of periods (amenorrhea). This results in a loss of oestrogen that can cause bone loss at a time when girls should be increasing their bone mass. It is crucial to see a doctor or dietitian if there has been any menstrual cycle interruption.

Both boys and girls between the ages of 10 and 20 need around 1,300mg of calcium per day.

Early adulthood: 20–30 years
Bones will reach their peak strength during these years, but the body is no longer forming new bone as readily as before. Both men and women need at least 1,000mg of calcium per day and should aim to include weight-bearing exercise such as a brisk walk for at least 30 minutes on four or more days per week. Strength activities should also be incorporated at least two days per week.

Middle adulthood: 30–50 years
After you reach peak bone mass, gradual bone loss will start to occur. Remodelling is the process whereby your body is constantly removing old bone and rebuilding and replacing with new bone. Up to the age of 40, all the bone that has been removed has been replaced. After 40, however, less bone is replaced. At this life stage it is crucial to get enough calcium (at

least 1,000mg per day) and vitamin D as well as incorporating weight-bearing exercises into your daily routine.

Over-50s and menopausal women

The daily calcium recommendation remains the same for men at 1,000mg per day.

For women, it may be a good idea at this life stage to undergo a DEXA scan to measure your bone density. Some women may need to take medication in order to support their bones.

Women aged over 50 are currently recommended to take in 1,200mg calcium per day alongside 800IU of vitamin D, according to the National Osteoporosis Society. When taking a supplement, it is important to remember that they are just that – supplements. We should also be aiming to include calcium in our diet each day.

As women enter the menopausal transition, they lose around 10 per cent of their bone, and this figure can increase to 20 per cent in 'fast bone losers'. After around five years of early menopausal symptoms, bone loss slows but bone continues to be lost, just at a slower rate.

Why does this happen? Bone metabolism is under the influence of oestrogen. During menopause, oestrogen levels decline, and when oestrogen falls, there is a reduction in the production of new bone cells and an increase of bone resorption. This results in bones that are less dense, weaker and more susceptible to fracture.

Over-70s

Both men and women should now get 1,200mg of calcium per day. After they reach the age of 70, men are now more likely to experience fractures due to lower bone mass.

Calcium is just the beginning

Diet and physical activity both have an important role to play during all stages of life in supporting bone health. Adequate nutrition for bone health includes incorporating protein, polyunsaturated fatty acids, calcium and vitamin D. In this chapter, you will find lots of useful recipes that contain various nutrients and minerals to support healthy bones.

Salmon and salsa pitta pockets

Bone health

Hormonal health

Pregnancy and fertility

Skin health

Serves 4

Prep: 10 minutes + 2 hours marinating

Cook: 10 minutes

Nutrients per serving

Calories (kcal) **380**

Carbohydrate **36**

Protein (g) **27**

Fat (g) **14**

Ingredients

4 salmon fillets
1 tbsp maple syrup
1 tbsp smoked paprika
1 tsp ground cumin
½ lemon, juiced
4 wholemeal pitta pockets
iceberg lettuce, sliced
4 tbsp low-fat mayonnaise
1 tsp paprika

For the salsa:
1 medium-sized pineapple, peeled and finely diced
¼ red onion, chopped
1 tbsp coriander, fresh or dried
1 lime, juiced
salt and pepper

This recipe can be enjoyed by the whole family and is delicious served warm or cold. Salmon is one of the rare food sources of vitamin D and is high in omega-3. These pitta pockets are packed with flavour and have a gorgeous crunchy texture. If you have the time I would recommend letting the salmon marinate overnight in the fridge but if you are short on time it's not necessary!

1 Put the salmon fillets in a large dish. Mix together the maple syrup, paprika, cumin and lemon juice in a small bowl. Spread evenly over the salmon fillets and place in the fridge for at least 2 hours.

2 To make the salsa, combine the salsa ingredients in a small bowl and season to taste with salt and pepper.

3 Heat the grill to high. Grill the salmon fillets, skin side up, for 4–5 minutes until the skin is crisp. Turn them over and grill for another 4–5 minutes until cooked through.

4 Mix together the mayonnaise and paprika. Assemble the pitta pockets with lettuce, salsa, salmon and mayonnaise.

Roasted fig fruit bowl

Bone health   Gut health   Immune health   Vegetarian

Serves 2

Prep: 5 minutes

Cook: 15 minutes

Nutrients per serving

Calories (kcal) **280**

Carbohydrate **45**

Protein (g) **16.5**

Fat (g) **3**

Ingredients

4 large figs, washed and cut into halves
2 tbsp honey
juice of ¼ lemon
½ tsp ground cinnamon
handful of blueberries
300g Greek yoghurt
1 kiwi, sliced
2 tbsp unsalted pistachio nuts

Figs are a great source of bone-friendly minerals including magnesium, phosphorus and calcium, which work together to improve bone density. Five medium-sized figs contain approximately 90mg of calcium, and they are also a source of magnesium, a mineral that helps the body absorb and retain calcium in the bones. Greek yoghurt is a source of calcium and probiotics and this breakfast is bursting with antioxidants from fresh (or frozen) fruit.

1 Preheat the oven to 200°C/180°C fan/gas mark 6. Cut the figs into halves and place cut-side up on a lined non-stick baking tray.

2 In a small bowl whisk the honey, lemon juice and cinnamon until combined. Spoon the mixture over the figs and roast in the oven for 15 minutes.

3 Scatter the blueberries over the figs and return to the oven for 2 more minutes.

4 Divide the yoghurt between 2 bowls and top with the roasted fruit and any juices from the roasting tray. Add the sliced kiwi and pistachio nuts and enjoy.

Superfood smoothie bowl

Bone health

Gut health

Immune health

Vegetarian

Serves 1

Prep: 5 minutes

Nutrients per serving

Calories (kcal) **410**

Carbohydrate **40**

Protein (g) **11**

Fat (g) **24**

Ingredients

1 banana, frozen
handful of ice cubes
150g Greek yoghurt
100ml unsweetened almond milk
1 tsp maca powder
1 tbsp almond butter
1 tbsp honey
toppings of your choice, e.g.
   toasted nuts, coconut flakes,
   berries, bee pollen

While I was in Australia I made or ate smoothie bowls nearly every day, for breakfast, as an afternoon snack or after dinner. They are a great way to pack in essential nutrients and you can include whatever toppings you like. Maca powder, which has a caramel flavour, is a rich source of amino acids, calcium and minerals. Recent research has looked at its role in preventing osteoporosis and arthritis.

1 Blend together all of the ingredients in a food processor until smooth.
2 Add to a bowl and top with your favourite toppings – I used coconut flakes, toasted flaked almonds, berries, bee pollen and some edible flowers.

Chicken bone broth

Bone health

Gut health

Immune health

Skin health

Serves 4

Prep: 10 minutes

Cook: 50 minutes

Nutrients per serving

Calories (kcal) **260**

Carbohydrates (g) **22**

Protein (g) **10**

Fat (g) **4**

Ingredients

1 chicken carcass
1 large onion, sliced
1 tbsp apple cider vinegar
2 bay leaves
1 tsp dried rosemary
2 garlic cloves, chopped
1 carrot, chopped
1 celery stick, chopped
2 vermicelli noodle nests, to serve
salt and pepper

Bone broth provides important nutrients, especially minerals, to support healthy bones. Simmering the bones with a dash of vinegar helps release the nutrients from the bone marrow, which is rich in iron, vitamins A and K, selenium and zinc. When you've made a roast chicken, or any dish that uses a whole chicken, reserve the carcass to make this delicious, nutritious broth.

1 Put all the ingredients, apart from the noodles, in a large pan. Add 1.5 litres of water, cover with a lid and simmer for 40 minutes.
2 Place a sieve or colander over a large bowl and pour the broth through the sieve.
3 Return the broth to the pan and add the vermicelli noodles. Cook for 5 minutes until the noodles are soft. Season with a pinch of salt and pepper and serve warm.

Lime and black bean prawns with brown rice

Bone health

Gut health

Heart health

Serves 4

Prep: 5 minutes

Cook: 30 minutes

Nutrients per serving

Calories (kcal) **305**

Carbohydrate **36**

Protein (g) **28**

Fat (g) **4**

Ingredients

1 tbsp olive oil
400g raw prawns, peeled
3 garlic cloves, minced

For the rice:
480ml vegetable stock
280g brown rice
juice of 1 lime
400g black beans
1 tbsp fresh coriander, chopped,
    plus extra to serve
½ tsp cayenne pepper
lime wedges, to serve

This recipe can be enjoyed in tacos, burritos or on its own. Black beans are a source of calcium and phosphorus, which play an important role in bone structure, as well as iron and zinc, which help to maintain strength and elasticity in bones and joints. The phytate in beans can cause digestive discomfort or bloating, so if you are using dried beans, try soaking your beans in water for 30 minutes before cooking to reduce the phytate level.

1 Heat the olive oil in a large frying pan over a medium heat. Add the prawns and garlic and cook for 3–4 minutes or until the prawns are pink. Remove the prawns and garlic from the pan and set aside.

2 Put the vegetable stock and rice in a saucepan, bring to the boil and stir for 2 minutes. Reduce the heat, cover the saucepan with a lid and simmer for 15–20 minutes until the rice is cooked through. You may need to add a little water if the rice looks too dry.

3 Mix in the lime juice, black beans, coriander and cayenne pepper and stir.

4 Add the prawns to the rice and black bean mixture and heat through over a low heat, stirring continuously for 1–2 minutes, and serve warm with an extra sprinkling of fresh coriander and some lime wedges for squeezing.

Mexican chicken salad

Bone health

Fitness

Serves 2

Prep: 5 minutes

Cook: 20 minutes

Nutrients per serving

Calories (kcal) **551**

Carbohydrate **39**

Protein (g) **35**

Fat (g) **26**

Ingredients

1 tsp olive oil

2 skinless, boneless chicken breasts

100g quinoa

1 red pepper, chopped

180g tinned sweetcorn

200g kidney beans

1 red onion, diced

½ cucumber, sliced

2 tbsp jalapeños, sliced

½ romaine lettuce, cut into bite-size pieces

For the dressing:

2 tbsp olive oil

juice of 1 lime

½ tsp Tabasco sauce

¼ tsp smoked paprika

½ tsp salt

¼ tsp black pepper

If you're looking to spice up your lunch menu, give this recipe a go. I like to serve this salad with some crunchy tortilla chips, but they are an optional add-on. Studies show that higher protein intake helps to maintain bone mineral density, and chicken is a great source of lean protein. This recipe also contains bone-building beans and healthy fats from avocados.

1 Preheat oven to 200°C/180°C fan/gas mark 6, and line a baking tray with baking paper. Drizzle the olive oil over the chicken breasts and transfer them to the tray. Bake chicken in the preheated oven for 16–18 minutes until cooked through.

2 While the chicken is cooking, place the quinoa in a small saucepan and add 200ml of water. Bring to a boil, then cover the pan, reduce the heat to low and let it cook for 15–18 minutes until the water has evaporated and the quinoa is cooked through. Drain the quinoa and add to two serving bowls.

3 Mix all the dressing ingredients in a bowl and whisk until smooth. Set aside.

4 Add the pepper, sweetcorn, beans, onion, cucumber, jalapeños and lettuce to the quinoa bowls and top with cooked chicken. Drizzle the dressing over and serve warm.

Tomato chicken pasta bake

Bone health

Cognitive health

Fitness

Serves 6

Prep: 5 minutes

Cook: 55 minutes

Nutrients per serving

Calories (kcal) **320**

Carbohydrate **42**

Protein (g) **18**

Fat (g) **8**

Ingredients

1 tbsp olive oil
1 shallot, finely chopped
2 garlic cloves, thinly sliced
800g tinned chopped tomatoes
80g spinach
1 tbsp fresh or dried basil, chopped
300g wholewheat penne
4 skinless chicken breasts, sliced
    into strips
100g mozzarella, sliced
50g grated Parmesan

Pasta, chicken and cheese are good sources of calcium, which is an essential mineral for building and maintaining strong bones. Tomatoes are rich in lycopene, a powerful antioxidant that may help reduce the risk of bone fractures. I love to cook this dish if I am hosting a dinner party as it comes together very easily and is always a crowd pleaser.

1 Preheat oven to 200°C/180°C fan/gas mark 6.
2 Heat the oil in a large frying pan over a medium heat and gently fry the shallot for 10 minutes. Add the garlic and cook for another minute. Add the tomatoes, spinach and basil, stir well and simmer, uncovered, for 15 minutes.
3 Meanwhile, cook the pasta according to the instructions on the packet.
4 Fill a large saucepan with water and bring to the boil. Add the chicken strips and simmer for 10–12 minutes, drain and put the chicken pieces in a casserole dish along with the cooked pasta.
5 Pour over the tomato sauce and add the mozzarella on top. Cover with grated Parmesan and bake in the preheated oven for 15–20 minutes until bubbling and golden brown.

Thai-style butternut tofu curry

Bone health

Hormonal health

Vegan

Serves 4

Prep: 5 minutes

Cook: 30 minutes

Nutrients per serving

Calories (kcal) **390**

Carbohydrate **35**

Protein (g) **15**

Fat (g) **19**

Ingredients

1 tbsp olive oil
1 brown onion, chopped
1 tbsp ginger, grated
1 garlic clove, minced
500g butternut squash, cubed
400ml coconut milk
200ml vegetable stock
2 tbsp fresh lime juice
2 tbsp fish sauce (or use soy sauce
   to make it vegan)
1 tbsp red curry paste
2 tsp caster sugar
450g firm tofu, drained and cut into
   cubes
60g spinach
2 tbsp sliced fresh basil, plus extra
   to serve (optional)
280g brown rice, to serve

Many of my friends have dietary restrictions, and this recipe ticks the vegetarian-friendly, dairy-free and gluten-free boxes, but is full of fibre, magnesium, phosphorus, vitamin K and potassium. I like to serve it with brown rice, which is a good source of calcium and magnesium. It can be stored in an airtight container in the fridge for three days.

1   Heat the oil in a large pot over medium heat. Add the chopped onion, ginger and garlic and stir until fragrant (about 2 minutes). Add the cubed butternut squash and stir for 1 minute.

2   Add the coconut milk, vegetable stock, lime juice, fish sauce (or soy sauce), curry paste and sugar and bring to a simmer.

3   Stir in the tofu and simmer for 20 minutes or until the squash is tender. Add in the spinach and fresh basil and cook until wilted, about 2 minutes.

4   Meanwhile, cook the rice according to the instructions on the packet. To serve, spoon the curry over the rice and top with extra basil, if desired.

Cherry Basque cheesecake with cherry coulis

 Bone health Heart health Vegetarian

Serves 12

Prep: 15 minutes, plus 4 hours cooling time

Cook: 45 minutes

Nutrients per serving

Calories (kcal) **470**

Carbohydrate **19**

Protein (g) **8**

Fat (g) **26**

Ingredients

800g cream cheese
150g caster sugar
50g light brown sugar
35g plain flour
100g sour cream
5 eggs, beaten
1 tsp vanilla extract
handful of fresh or frozen black cherries

For the cherry coulis:

300g fresh or frozen black cherries
50g caster sugar
50ml amaretto

Basque cheesecake has a soft centre and a crisp, slightly caramelised top, and it always goes down a storm. The heroes of this recipe are the cherries. Studies have shown that antioxidants in cherries help reduce pain and inflammation from osteoarthritis, and some people take cherry supplements to help improve bone mineral density. They provide a key bone-building mineral – silicon – and they are delicious!

1 Preheat the oven to 220°C/200°C fan/gas mark 7. Place two large squares of baking paper on top of each other to make a large star shape and place into a high-sided 20cm cake tin. The paper should be twice the height of the tin.

2 Put the cream cheese and both sugars in a mixing bowl and mix until smooth and creamy. Add the flour, sour cream, eggs and vanilla and mix together until smooth. Add the cherries and mix gently until combined.

3 Pour into the cake tin and bake in the oven for 40–45 minutes. When it comes out of the oven it may look slightly burnt but that is just the caramelisation! It should also wobble slightly. It is important to let it stand at room temperature for at least 4 hours after you take it out of the oven.

4 To make the coulis, put all the ingredients in a saucepan and heat over a low–medium heat for 1–2 minutes. Then turn up the heat and let it bubble and thicken for 10 minutes. Blitz in a food processor or mixer until smooth and drizzle over the cheesecake.

Kale chips

Bone health | Cognitive health | Gut health | Hormonal health | Skin health | Pregnancy and fertility | Vegan

Serves 4

Prep: 5 minutes

Cook: 10 minutes

Nutrients per serving

Calories (kcal) **65**

Carbohydrate **6**

Protein (g) **2.5**

Fat (g) **4**

Ingredients

280g raw kale
1 tbsp olive or sesame oil
½ tsp sea salt (optional)
2 tbsp nutritional yeast (optional)

My mum first made these for me years ago. I wasn't a fan of kale and when she told me what they were made of I didn't believe her! Kale is a great source of calcium and vitamin K, which plays a significant role in bone health by boosting osteotrophic (bone formation and strengthening) activity, and vitamin C supports collagen production. If you want a healthy alternative to shop-bought crisps, do give them a go!

1 Preheat the oven to 220°C/200°C fan/gas mark 7.
2 Wash and trim the kale, tearing out the stems and ribs. Rip the leaves into bite-size pieces.
3 Line a baking tray with baking paper and lay the kale leaves flat onto the paper. Drizzle with the oil and toss the leaves around with your fingers to distribute it evenly.
4 Bake for 5 minutes, then remove from the oven, turn the kale over and bake for 5 more minutes until browned and crisp.
5 Remove from oven and sprinkle with sea salt and nutritional yeast if desired.

Pregnancy and fertility

Diet plays an important role in trying to conceive. Eating a balanced diet can help optimise fertility and increase the chances of getting pregnant. For some couples, pregnancy can happen instantaneously but for many others it can be a long and challenging journey. We can't always control our circumstances but what we can control is how we cope with and react to challenges we are faced with. Looking at your diet and lifestyle is an often overlooked but crucial step in navigating that journey.

Trying to conceive (TTC)

Folic acid

The HSE recommends that all women of child-bearing age take a daily folic acid supplement of 400mcg daily, even if they are not planning for a baby. The reason behind this is that nearly half of all pregnancies in Ireland are unplanned. Folate cannot be stored in the body and in order to have sufficient levels at the time of conception, supplementation should commence at least three months before conception. Folic acid should be continued for the first 12 weeks of pregnancy and can be safely stopped after the first trimester.

Manufactured folic acid is converted in the body into folate, a B-group vitamin. Our bodies need folate to make DNA and other genetic material, and in unborn babies it plays a role in nervous system development. During the first few weeks of pregnancy the neural tube closes and fuses; this later becomes the baby's brain and spinal cord. A neural tube defect (NTD) is more likely to occur if mothers do not have enough folate before or during the first few weeks of pregnancy. Sadly, not all NTDs can be prevented, but taking a folic acid is helpful in most pregnancies.

Coenzyme Q10

Sperm and egg development and maturation are complex processes that require a large amount of energy and are subject to oxidative damage. Coenzyme Q10 (CoQ10) is an antioxidant that our bodies naturally produce and is used by cells for growth and maintenance. Levels of CoQ10 naturally decline as we age. It has been widely used as a dietary supplement to support various health conditions such as heart conditions, diabetes, statin-induced muscle weakness and migraines. Interestingly, recent research has looked at the role of CoQ10 in supporting male and female fertility.

How CoQ10 can help to support fertility:
1 It acts as a powerful antioxidant and protects cells from the damaging effects of free radicals on our reproductive system.
2 It is an important part of the electron transport chain, which is responsible for generating energy in our cells. With a higher amount of energy within cells, processes like sperm and egg development can be carried out more efficiently.

It is well documented that fertility declines

with age, more specifically the number of eggs available to be fertilised (ovarian reserve) as well as the quality of the eggs. A 2015 study showed that suboptimal levels of CoQ10 can lead to oocyte deficits and age-associated decline in fertility. The study also concluded that CoQ10 can help support egg quality as we age.

If you are eating a balanced and varied diet you could consume between 3mg and 6mg of CoQ10 a day. Food sources include beef, chicken, pork, trout, spinach, cauliflower and broccoli. Fertility clinics will prescribe doses between 100mg and 600mg daily. Smaller concentrations can be found in over-the-counter supplements, but if it is something you want further information on you can talk to your doctor about it.

What about men?
The concentration in blood samples of CoQ10 has been correlated with sperm motility, morphology and concentration. Some studies have demonstrated improvements in these parameters, but more research is needed to further clarify its role.

Alcohol
It takes around 2–4 months to improve the quality of our eggs. That is why it is recommended to abstain from alcohol at least three months before trying to conceive. When it comes to an occasional drink, the evidence is mixed. Some studies have found that drinking a moderate amount of alcohol can increase the risk of infertility. Conversely, a study published in *Fertility and Sterility* in 2017 showed that low-level red wine consumption was associated with increased ovarian reserve among women with regular menstrual periods. Red wine contains a compound called resveratrol, which has anti-inflammatory properties. When it comes to women with hormonal conditions

such as PCOS it is recommended to cut out alcohol entirely in order to successfully ovulate and conceive.

Drinking alcohol at any stage of pregnancy can cause long-term health problems for the baby. It is linked to the development of foetal alcohol spectrum disorders, a group of conditions that can include physical problems and problems with behaviour and learning.

Alcohol can also decrease male fertility. As well as affecting hormone levels, it can affect the function of the testes, inhibiting sperm from developing properly and reducing the sperm's ability to move towards the egg. This is because alcohol stops the liver from efficiently metabolising vitamin A, which is needed for sperm development.

Stress
Speaking from personal experience I know all too well how unhelpful it is when people say, 'Just relax and it will happen for you.' Of course, nobody means any malice when they offer that wisdom, but when you have spent months or years trying to conceive it really is the last thing you want to hear. Even knowing everything I knew about the effects of stress on the reproductive system it took me a long time to finally reverse my mindset. Failing to conceive can be stressful. Deal with those emotions. Then come back stronger and lean on family and friends. Your miracle will come to you in time. Look after your mind and body and nourish yourself well with nutritious food.

If you and your partner have been trying to conceive for 12 months or more it might be worth seeking out advice from fertility specialists.

Additional calories

Since becoming pregnant myself I have lost count of the number of people who have told me that I am now 'eating for two'. This old wives' tale is actually a myth and while there is an increase in daily calorie consumption, it is not quite double portions! For the average healthy pregnant woman with no underlying health conditions, your calorie intake should increase gradually during pregnancy. During the first trimester, the focus should be on choosing balanced, nutritious foods. You don't require any additional calories during this time. That being said, my appetite grew exponentially and I listened to my body and increased my snacks and meals until I felt satisfied. It is an excellent time to focus on nourishing yourself, consuming a varied mix of foods, including macro- and micronutrients, and also staying well hydrated.

Moving into the second trimester you can increase your daily calorie consumption by 300–350 calories per day. Finally, during the third trimester and throughout breastfeeding an extra 500 calories per day is advised. These extra calories can come from a few additional snacks or one additional meal per day depending on how often you feel hungry and what your own personal food preference is.

Protein
1 serving = 50–75g cooked meat, 100g fish, 6 dessertspoons of legumes or 2 eggs
Recommended intake per day: minimum 2 servings

Protein is the building block of our bodies. Our protein requirements increase during pregnancy in order to build maternal and foetal tissues. The International Federation of Gynaecology and Obstetrics (FIGO) recommends increasing protein by 10–25g per day during trimesters 2 and 3, aiming for roughly 70–85g per day. Protein helps to increase the satiety of meals, helps to stabilise blood sugar and makes you feel fuller for longer. Gestational diabetes is prevalent in Ireland, so maintaining stable blood sugar and insulin levels is important throughout your pregnancy. Never eat undercooked, raw or cured meats, liver or high-mercury fish (swordfish or too much tuna) during your pregnancy.
Sources include: red meats, chicken, turkey, eggs, legumes.

Carbohydrates
1 serving = 1 fistful of vegetables, starchy grains, 1 cupped palm of fruit, 1 slice of bread, 1 medium potato
Recommended intake per day: 6 servings

Carbohydrates are a fundamental part of our diet and are the body's fuel of choice. They are essential for hormonal health, growing your baby and any additional exercise you may be doing. Try to focus on obtaining the majority of your carbohydrates from vegetables, fruit and whole grains as they are a rich source of fibre, vitamins and overall have a higher nutrition content.
Sources include: fruit, vegetables, potatoes, sweet potatoes, rice, bread, pasta and pulses.

Fibre
1 serving = 1 medium pear, 1 apple (including skin), 90g broccoli, 1 medium potato (including skin)

The HSE recommends getting 18–30g of fibre a day, particularly if you are suffering from constipation. Constipation and haemorrhoids are common during pregnancy, so increasing your fibre and water intake can help to relieve symptoms.

Sources include: raspberries, green peas, oats, lentils, black beans, chia seeds.

Fats

1 serving = 1 tbsp olive oil / rapeseed oil for cooking
Recommended per day = 2 portions

The polyunsaturated fats omega-3 and omega-6 are the building blocks of our fat-based tissues, like our brain and cell membranes, as well as precursors to important hormones. According to FIGO, fats should account for 15–30 per cent of your daily nutrition during pregnancy (no increase or decrease from pre-pregnancy). Omega-3 fatty acids make up a large part of our brain; 60 per cent is composed of omega-3 DHA, which is a type found in fish. Before birth, up to 75 per cent of your baby's brain cells are already in place, and the remainder will be in place by the end of their first year. As well as brain development, omegas are necessary for normal eye development.

There have also been some recent interesting studies looking at the role of omega-3 fatty acids in fighting pre-natal depression. This could be explained by their contribution to healthier cell membranes, allowing serotonin to flow better between cells, but it's an area of research that is still being explored and the reasons are not yet fully understood. It is recommended to eat two portions of fish per week, ideally one of them should be oily fish. It is a good source of protein and is rich in omega-3 fats, selenium, zinc, B12 and iodine. Oily fish are also a source of vitamins D and A.
Sources include: oily fish such as sardines, salmon, mackerel, trout, white fish such as cod and plaice, walnuts, flaxseed and linseed, avocados.

Omegas

Omega-3 and omega-6 are essential fatty acids, meaning that our body cannot make them, so we must obtain them through our diet or a supplement.

Research has shown that the potential long-term benefits to your baby of omega-3 during pregnancy include:

- **A healthy birth weight**
- **Reduced risk of pre-term delivery**
- **Reduced risk of your baby developing eczema later in life**
- **Healthier, stronger bones**

Omega-3 is particularly important during the later stages of pregnancy. So if you do not consume fish in your diet, it may be an idea to consider a supplement throughout the last trimester.

Iron

As your pregnancy progresses your blood volume increases, and this may make you feel fatigued. Iron is needed to produce new blood cells in your developing baby. The HSE recommend that pregnant women eat two sources of iron per day and should aim to get a mix of haem and non-haem iron. Non-haem iron is less easily absorbed by the body. Haem iron is found in red meats and non-haem iron is found in spinach and other dark green leafy vegetables, eggs and pulses. As previously mentioned, vitamin C helps with the absorption of iron, so it is a good idea to consume your iron-rich foods with a vitamin C-rich source such as berries, kiwis and oranges. Aim to consume around 75mg of vitamin C daily to support immune health and overall health and well-being.

Calcium

Calcium should be another staple in your pregnancy diet. It is important for the growth of your baby's developing bones. The HSE recommends at least three helpings of hard cheese, milk or dairy per day as they are a rich source of calcium.

Hydration

Our bodies are made up of approximately 60 per cent water, according to the HSE. Two to three litres of water per day is adequate to meet the average woman's hydration status. During pregnancy blood volume increases by up to 50 per cent, which means that you will need more water. If you are exercising during your pregnancy this is an additional reason to stay on top of hydration. It is important for women during the first trimester not to get overheated while exercising, so having water with you during training is imperative!

Caffeine

When we hear the word 'caffeine', coffee instantly springs to mind, but caffeine is present in more foods than we might realise: 130g of dark chocolate contains around 30mg of caffeine; one cup (230ml) of black tea contains 48mg and one cup (8oz) of drip coffee contains approximately 137mg (for reference a Starbucks 'tall' coffee = 12oz).

So what does the research say? Well, the studies are mixed. Some suggest that high caffeine consumption during pregnancy can result in pre-term birth and intrauterine growth restriction (IUGR). The American Congress of Obstetricians and Gynecologists states that 'moderate consumption (<200mg per day) does not appear to be a major contributing factor in miscarriage or pre-term birth'. The relationship between caffeine and IUGR is still unclear.

It is always better to be on the safe side and be mindful of caffeine intake.

Do what feels good for you

It can be incredibly overwhelming trying to follow the tidal wave of dos and don'ts when it comes to pregnancy. They are simply guidelines and at the end of the day this is your time to nourish your body and grow your baby. If you're feeling hungry, eat.

Foods to avoid

Raw fish, undercooked or cured meats, soft cheeses and unpasteurised milk should all be avoided during pregnancy since they carry the risk of listeriosis, salmonella or food poisoning.

Foods high in vitamin A such as pâté, liver and haggis should also be avoided as they can cause harm to the foetus if consumed in high amounts. Foods high in lead and mercury can damage the developing neurological system and should be avoided. Fish such as mackerel and swordfish fall into this group, along with large amounts of tuna, which should be restricted. Another one to be mindful of is the type of water bottle you drink out from: make sure you have one that is lead-and BPA-free.

French toast

Pregnancy and fertility

Bone health

Fitness

Vegetarian

Serves 2

Prep: 5 minutes
Cook: 10 minutes

Nutrients per serving

Calories (kcal) **250**

Carbohydrates (g) **35**

Protein (g) **15**

Fat (g) **6**

Ingredients

2 egg whites
200ml milk of choice
1 tsp ground cinnamon
1 tsp ground nutmeg
1 tsp vanilla extract
2 tbsp maple syrup
juice and zest of ½ orange
4 slices wholewheat bread
light cooking spray oil

I always crave something sweet in the morning and this healthier version of French toast is so flavourful and can be served with fresh fruit and Greek yoghurt or on its own. It provides a good serving of both carbohydrates and protein to help keep hunger levels at bay.

1 Put the egg whites, milk, cinnamon, nutmeg, vanilla extract, maple syrup and orange juice and zest in a bowl and whisk together until combined.
2 Dip the bread in the mixture, one slice at a time, to coat and set aside.
3 Spray some light cooking spray oil into a large frying pan and add the soaked bread slices to the pan. Cook for 2–3 minutes on one side and then flip and cook for 2–3 minutes on the other side.

Strawberry and banana baked oats

Pregnancy and fertility   Heart health   Hormonal health   Vegetarian

Makes 8 servings

Prep: 5 minutes

Cook: 35 minutes

Nutrients per serving

Calories (kcal) **320**

Carbohydrates (g) **40**

Protein (g) **8**

Fat (g) **12**

Ingredients

1 tbsp coconut oil, melted, or light
    cooking spray oil
200g rolled oats
1 tsp baking powder
2 eggs
60ml maple syrup
350ml milk of choice
1 tsp vanilla extract
300g strawberries, halved
2 bananas, peeled and chopped

Oats are one of my go-to breakfast meals. They provide a slow release of energy and don't cause big spikes in blood sugar levels. This is a good meal prep recipe to make on a Sunday evening and store in an airtight container to warm through for breakfast during the week. You can add whatever fruit you like.

1 Preheat the oven to 200°C/180°C fan/gas mark 6 and lightly grease a baking dish with melted coconut oil or light cooking spray oil.

2 Put the oats and baking powder in a bowl and mix to combine.

3 Add the eggs, maple syrup, milk, vanilla extract, half the strawberries and all the bananas to the oats and mix until everything is combined.

4 Pour the mixture into the baking dish, add the remaining strawberries on top and bake in the oven for 30–35 minutes.

Turkey flatbread

Pregnancy and fertility

Bone health

Heart health

Fitness

Serves 2

Prep: 10 minutes

Cook: 10 minutes

Nutrients per serving

Calories (kcal) **440**

Protein (g) **39.5**

Carbohydrates (g) **15**

Fat (g) **26**

Ingredients

2 wholewheat wraps
200g tinned chopped tomatoes
1 tbsp tomato purée
1 tsp dried oregano
1 red pepper, roasted and sliced
100g sliced or shredded cooked
    turkey breast
100g grated Cheddar

For the cottage cheese dip:
150g pasteurised cottage cheese
1 tsp fresh chives, chopped
½ lemon, juiced
1 tsp garlic powder
black pepper, to taste

Pizza was one of my cravings throughout the first trimester, but eating a pizza every day would not have been very nutritious for me or the baby! This turkey flatbread is a source of lean protein and dairy and is a quick, satisfying lunch. The dip, rich in calcium, phosphorus, folate and vitamin B12 – all essential for pregnant women – also goes well with carrots and crackers as a snack.

1 Preheat the oven to 200°C/180°C fan/gas mark 6.
2 In a small bowl, combine the chopped tomatoes, tomato purée and oregano and mix until combined.
3 Put the wraps on a baking tray sprayed with oil or a sheet of tinfoil and use the back of a spoon to spread the tomato base evenly across them. Top with the roasted red pepper, shredded turkey and grated cheese and place in the oven for 10 minutes or until the edges are golden and crisp.
4 Remove from the oven, slice and season with some black pepper
5 To make the dip, add all the ingredients to a food processor and blend until smooth.

Sweet potato and cheese frittata

Pregnancy and fertility

Cognitive health

Fitness

Vegetarian

Serves 2–3

Prep: 20 minutes

Cook: 30 minutes

Nutrients per serving

Calories (kcal) **310**

Carbohydrates (g) **16**

Protein (g) **20**

Fat (g) **16**

Ingredients

1 small sweet potato, cubed
olive oil
6 eggs
20ml milk
1 tsp baking powder
1 tsp turmeric
4 spring onions, chopped
handful of baby spinach leaves
30g Cheddar cheese, grated

Eggs are a great source of protein as well as choline, which is an essential nutrient for the baby's developing brain. This frittata is really quick and easy to make if you're short on time. I like to make it on a Sunday and bring slices into work for lunch or an afternoon snack.

1. Preheat the oven to 200°C/180°C fan/gas mark 6. Put the sweet potato on a baking tray, drizzle with oil and roast in the oven for 18–20 minutes.

2. Heat the grill to high. Whisk together the eggs, milk, baking powder, turmeric and chopped spring onions. Add half the Cheddar, the sweet potato cubes and spinach and mix to combine.

3. Drizzle 1 tbsp oil into an ovenproof non-stick frying pan. Pour in the egg mixture and cook for 8–10 minutes until the eggs are nearly set. Place the frying pan under a hot grill for one minute until the frittata is fully cooked through. Sprinkle over the remaining cheese to serve.

Nourishing veggie bowl

Pregnancy and fertility

Immune health

Gut health

Skin health

Vegan

Serves 2

Prep: 15 minutes

Cook: 25 minutes

Nutrients per serving

Calories (kcal) **500**

Carbohydrates (g) **38**

Protein (g) **15**

Fat (g) **30**

Ingredients

80g wholewheat couscous
200ml vegetable stock
250g cauliflower, cut into small florets
1 carrot, sliced
1 tbsp olive oil
1 tsp ground cumin
200g tinned chickpeas, drained and rinsed
1 tsp smoked paprika
large handful of spinach leaves
black pepper
2 tbsp pumpkin or sunflower seeds

For the dressing:
1 tsp harissa paste
1 tsp lemon juice
½ tbsp olive oil
1 tbsp water

This is a quick and easy lunch that provides a good helping of vitamins, minerals and antioxidants to support you and your growing baby. Iron is provided by sunflower seeds and spinach, carrots are a great source of vitamin C (which helps the body absorb iron) and plant-based protein comes from the couscous and chickpeas.

1 Put the couscous in a bowl and pour over the vegetable stock, cover with a large plate or tea towel and leave to absorb the stock (about 10 minutes).

2 Preheat oven to 220°C/200°C fan/gas mark 7 and lightly grease a baking tray. Put the cauliflower and carrot on the tray, drizzle with ½ tbsp of olive oil and sprinkle with cumin. Roast for 15–18 minutes or until lightly browned.

3 In a small bowl mix the remaining ½ tbsp of olive oil with the paprika and add the chickpeas to the bowl to coat. Take the tray out of the oven and scatter the chickpeas over the vegetables. Roast for another 5 minutes.

4 To make the dressing, put all the ingredients in a small bowl and whisk together.

5 Divide the spinach leaves between two bowls, add the couscous, then the roasted vegetables and chickpeas, drizzle with dressing and season with a pinch of black pepper. Scatter seeds on top to serve.

Cottage pie

Pregnancy and fertility

Heart health

Fitness

Serves 4

Prep: 40 minutes

Cook: 20 minutes

Nutrients per serving

Calories (kcal) **420**

Protein (g) **23**

Carbohydrates (g) **27**

Fat (g) **25**

Ingredients

1 tbsp olive oil plus a little for greasing
1 shallot, finely chopped
350g lean chicken mince
2 small carrots, finely chopped
2 sticks of celery, finely chopped
500ml chicken stock
black pepper
1 tsp dried parsley or 10g fresh parsley, leaves only
400g potatoes, peeled and cut into large chunks
50ml milk
1 tbsp Benecol spread
50g Cheddar, grated

Cottage pie is such a comforting and filling meal. It is also great for making ahead and storing in airtight containers or freezing for meals on the go. Potatoes are a good source of fibre, which is particularly important during pregnancy as hormones can cause the digestive system to slow down.

1 Preheat the oven to 200°C/180°C fan/gas mark 6 and grease a an ovenproof baking or casserole dish.
2 Heat the oil in a large pan and fry the shallot over a medium heat for 5 minutes.
3 Add the minced chicken and cook for 5 minutes, or until browned, then add the carrots and celery and cook for a further 5 minutes. Stir in the stock, season with black pepper, add the parsley and simmer for 30 minutes.
4 Meanwhile, put the potatoes in a saucepan of boiling salted water and cook until tender (approximately 20 minutes). Drain and mash with the milk and Benecol and beat until smooth and fluffy.
5 Spoon the chicken mixture into the prepared dish and cover with the mashed potatoes. Sprinkle over the cheese and bake for 20–25 minutes until golden brown.

Steamed yellow fish curry

Pregnancy and fertility

Cognitive health

Heart health

Serves 4

Prep: 15 minutes

Cook: 15 minutes

Nutrients per serving

Calories (kcal) **400**

Protein (g) **27**

Carbohydrates (g) **19.5**

Fat (g) **24**

Ingredients

1 tbsp sesame oil

1 red onion, peeled and cut into wedges

110g yellow curry paste

200ml light coconut milk

250g coconut cream

200g green beans, chopped

100g baby corn

4 skinless cod fillets, cut into chunks

juice of ½ lime

1 tbsp light brown sugar

2 tsp fish sauce

lime wedges, to serve

basmati, jasmine or steamed rice, to serve

Cod is an excellent source of protein, iron and zinc, which all are important nutrients to support growth and development. Cod is a safe choice in pregnancy as it is considered a low-mercury fish. It is also a source of those all-important omega-3 fatty acids – DHA in particular, which helps to support foetal brain and eye development. This is a fragrant, fresh, light dish that makes a lovely midweek dinner.

1 Heat the oil in a wok over medium heat. Add the onion wedges and fry for 2–3 minutes until lightly browned. Add the curry paste and fry for 1 minute until fragrant.
2 Stir in the coconut milk and coconut cream and bring to the boil. Reduce the heat to medium-low and add the green beans and baby corn. Add the fish and cook, gently stirring every 2 minutes, for 7–8 minutes.
3 Stir in the lime juice, sugar and fish sauce. Serve with rice of choice and lime wedges.

Turkey moussaka

Pregnancy and fertility

Gut health

Serves 4

Prep: 10 minutes

Cook: 60 minutes

Nutrients per serving

Calories (kcal) **410**

Carbohydrates (g) **10**

Protein (g) **48**

Fat (g) **18**

Ingredients

3 aubergines, cut into round slices
1 tbsp olive oil, plus extra for the
  aubergines
1 red onion, diced
2 garlic cloves, minced
600g lean turkey mince
400g tinned chopped tomatoes
1 tbsp tomato purée
200ml vegetable stock
2 tsp dried oregano
1 tsp dried basil
150g mozzarella
2 tbsp grated Parmesan
fresh basil, to serve (optional)

Aubergine contains a good amount of fibre to support the digestive system during pregnancy. It is also a source of folate, which is particularly important during the first trimester. Turkey is a lean protein and the dish contains a good mix of antioxidants, B vitamins and protein to keep you satisfied. It comes together quickly and most of the work is done in the oven, so sit back and relax!

1 Preheat the grill to high and arrange the aubergine slices in a single layer on a lined baking tray. Drizzle the aubergine slices with a little olive oil and grill for 2 minutes each side. Set aside.
2 Heat 1 tbsp olive oil in a large frying pan, add the onion and garlic and fry for 4–5 minutes at medium heat. Increase the heat to high, add the mince and fry for 5–6 minutes. Add the chopped tomatoes, tomato purée, stock, oregano and basil. Bring to a boil and simmer, uncovered, for 20 minutes.
3 Preheat the oven to 200°C/180°C fan/gas mark 6.
4 Grease a baking dish with 1 tbsp of oil or cooking spray oil and pour half of the turkey mixture into the dish. Layer with half the mozzarella and half of the aubergine slices. Repeat this process until you have used everything, finishing with aubergine slices. Sprinkle with Parmesan and bake in the oven for 30 minutes. Top with fresh basil leaves to serve, if desired.

White and dark chocolate mousse

Pregnancy and fertility

Vegetarian

Serves 4

Prep: 20 minutes, plus 1 hour chilling

Nutrients per serving

Calories (kcal) **375**

Protein (g) **11**

Carbohydrates (g) **23**

Fat (g) **27.5**

Ingredients

100g dark chocolate, chopped
250g low-fat cream cheese
100g white chocolate, chopped
2 tbsp caster sugar
1 tsp vanilla extract

One of my cravings throughout pregnancy was white chocolate. One of my favourite desserts is a chocolate mousse, but since most recipes contain raw egg I created one that is egg-free and can be eaten during pregnancy. I use cream cheese, but you can use whipped cream instead. While we should eat a varied nutrient-dense diet, we are also human, so never feel guilty about having the odd bit of chocolate!

1 Melt the dark chocolate in a heat-proof bowl over a saucepan of simmering water and add half of the cream cheese (125g). Remove from the heat and whisk well. In a second heat-proof bowl, melt the white chocolate and add the remaining cream cheese. Remove from the heat and whisk well.

2 Add ½ tsp of vanilla extract to each bowl and mix well. Taste for sweetness and add up to 1 tbsp of caster sugar to each bowl if the mixtures are not sweet enough.

3 Spoon the mixtures, alternating the dark and white, into 4 serving glasses. Use a knife to swirl the mixtures together and chill for at least an hour.

Anti-nausea smoothie

Pregnancy and fertility

Vegan

Serves 1

Prep: 5 minutes

Nutrients per serving

Calories (kcal) **380**

Protein (g) **11**

Fat (g) **14**

Carbohydrates (g) **36**

Ingredients

1 banana, sliced and frozen
60g frozen mango
2 tbsp peanut butter
1 tbsp chia seeds
50g baby spinach leaves
300ml almond milk

Smoothies are a great way to get nutrients into your diet when you can't tolerate certain foods. A balance of protein, fats and carbohydrates helps stabilise blood sugar. Packed with B vitamins, magnesium and protein, this smoothie can be enjoyed at any time of the day. I used to have it in the afternoon, when my nausea was worst, and whether placebo or not, it quickly became my go-to!

1 Put all ingredients in a blender and blitz until smooth.
2 Add ice for extra thickness or a spoon of honey or maple syrup for some sweetness.

Skin health

Our skin is so much more than just a covering. It is the body's largest organ, it is involved in thermal regulation and hormone exchange, and it is our first line of defence against pathogens – a key function in immune health. Our skin deserves a lot of attention, not because it is delicate and contributes to our appearance but because it is so important to our health. There are always new products on the market that promise to wash away wrinkles, make your skin glow like the sun and banish all your blemishes, and while skincare routines and the products we use topically on our skin are important for overall skin health, there is a natural option to consider first: our diet. The proteins, nutrients, antioxidants and minerals found in food support collagen production and healthy skin cell membranes. Food can also protect our skin from harmful pollutants and from ultraviolet (UV) rays. What you feed it on the inside will show on the outside.

Five food tips for healthy, glowing skin

1 Hydration

Do you ever notice that in the morning after a heavy night of alcohol, those little crows' feet and fine lines appear that bit more prominent? This is because alcohol causes dehydration. Our skin is composed of three layers: the outermost layer (epidermis); the underlying layer (dermis); and the subcutaneous tissue. If the epidermis doesn't contain enough water our skin can lose elasticity. Most of us underestimate the power of consuming enough water daily. Drinking enough water is the most natural way to get glowing and healthy skin. In addition, drinking water helps to flush away toxins. Toxins can clog pores, causing issues like spots and acne. The amount of water you should drink per day depends on your age, weight, height and activity levels but, generally speaking, health experts recommend drinking eight glasses or around two litres a day.

2 Healthy fats

Essential fatty acids like omega-3s and omega-6s are the building blocks of healthy cell membranes. These polyunsaturated fatty acids also help to produce the skin's natural oil barrier, which is important to keep skin hydrated and plump. Skin cells take about four weeks to form; they are pushed up, layer by layer, until they eventually reach the surface. As this process can take up to four weeks, it can take four weeks for changes in your diet to have a noticeable effect.

Every skin cell is surrounded by two fat layers that comprise the cell walls and is known as the phospholipid bilayer. This layer incorporates dietary fats and therefore gives the appearance of hydrated, healthy and plump skin.

Omega-3 fatty acids have anti-inflammatory properties which can have a positive impact on the skin, since inflammation can lead to many chronic skin conditions like acne and eczema. They also have the ability to suppress a hormone called insulin-like growth factor 1 (IGF-1), which can reduce the formation of spots and blemishes.

Good sources of healthy fats include fresh fish, especially salmon, sardines, mackerel, trout, tuna and halibut. Vegetarian sources of omega-3s include linseeds, walnuts, flaxseed, chia seeds and hemp seeds.

3 Incorporate lean protein sources

Lean protein sources include eggs, chicken and turkey. Red meat is one of the highest protein sources and contains the amino acids proline and glycine which studies have shown are involved in collagen synthesis. Red meat is also a good source of zinc, another key component of collagen synthesis. Collagen plays a vital role in skin health, as it is the main structural protein in the skin. It gives the skin strength and elasticity, helping to maintain its firmness. Collagen production naturally declines as we age, beginning in our late 20s or early 30s. As a result, the skin gradually loses its elasticity and firmness, leading to wrinkles, fine lines and sagging skin.

Bear in mind that red meat can be high in saturated fat and produces a chemical called trimethylamine N-oxide (TMAO), which has been linked to heart disease. When choosing red meats it's a good idea to look for lean, fat-free and unprocessed types.

4 Antioxidant-rich fruit

Antioxidants are compounds that help to prevent damage to cells by neutralising free radicals, which can damage skin cells, leading to premature ageing, wrinkles and skin problems. Antioxidants can also help to improve the overall health of the skin by promoting circulation, increasing hydration and supporting the skin's natural barrier function. They can also protect the skin from oxidative stress, which can lead to collagen breakdown and inflammation. Fruits and vegetables are one of the best sources of antioxidants, and in general the brighter the colour of the fruit or vegetable, the higher its antioxidant concentration. Every morning I try to incorporate into my oats at least two types of berry – blueberries, raspberries, strawberries – or grapes. Smoothies are another smart way to incorporate fruits and vegetables in the diet and they are preferable to juice because juicing tends to remove the outer skins, which contain all-important fibre. Tomatoes are rich in the antioxidant lycopene which has been studied for its ability to fight against sun damage. More research is needed in the area, but some studies have shown that lycopene can help protect skin against UV rays.

5 Beta-glucan

This polysaccharide and fibre is a bit of an unsung hero when it comes to skin health ingredients. Beta-glucan is found in the cell walls of certain foods, such as mushrooms and yeast. If you are taking it as a supplement, be sure to read the label to find out the formulation – beta (1,3) D-glucan is the bioactive form. Beta-glucan plays a role in immune response by helping the immune system to respond to stress or illness as well as decreasing unnecessary inflammation. Researchers have found glucan receptors in the skin and demonstrated how beta-glucan can impact collagen rebuilding after a wound. Food sources include oats, barley and mushrooms.

The gut–skin axis

Studies have shown that the gut microbiome (the collection of micro-organisms that reside in our guts) plays a role in the development of diseases beyond the digestive tract, including skin conditions like eczema, acne and psoriasis. The gut–skin axis refers to the bidirectional relationship between the microbiome and the skin. This relationship is regulated by inflammatory mediators and the immune system. Dysbiosis, or an imbalance of good versus bad bacteria, has been seen in certain inflammatory skin conditions like eczema, rosacea and psoriasis. Current research is looking at the role of probiotic supplementation for the treatment of certain inflammatory skin conditions. *Bifidobacterium*, *Lactobacillus* and *Streptococcus* are the most common species found in probiotics today. Certain lactobacilli strains such as *Lactobacillus paracasei* NCC2461 have been shown in some studies to improve the integrity of the skin barrier by improving skin sensitivity and preventing trans-epidermal water loss. In animal and human studies, the use of probiotics for conditions such as psoriasis seems promising and some studies report a decrease in symptom severity and number of relapses. *Bifidobacterium* appears to reduce skin sensitivity, while *Lactobacillus* may reduce skin inflammation and improve the skin's barrier function.

Stress, changes in the skin's pH levels, diet and chronic inflammation impact the diversity of microbes in your gut and can create an imbalance. When this imbalance occurs it can result in infections or skin conditions like eczema, acne or rosacea. Prebiotics and probiotics may help improve your skin's microbiome, so it can be helpful to try to include probiotic rich foods in your diet each day.

Vitamins and minerals

Vitamins and minerals play an important role in maintaining the health and appearance of the skin by promoting collagen production, supporting the skin barrier, reducing inflammation and providing antioxidant protection. You could be using the best skincare in the world but if you neglect your diet and vitamin intake you cannot begin to build the foundation of healthy skin.

Vitamin C
Vitamin C (ascorbic acid) plays an important role in maintaining skin health and can decrease melanin synthesis (overproduction of melanin can lead to pigmentation). It counteracts skin oxidation by fighting free radicals and has a role in the formation of the skin barrier and collagen in the dermis. Our bodies cannot make vitamin C, so it is important to obtain it daily from out diet.
Food sources include: bell peppers, oranges, strawberries, tomatoes, cauliflower, mangoes, Brussels sprouts and kiwis.

Vitamin D
Vitamin D is integral to skin health, playing a role in barrier maintenance and immune function. It also has anti-inflammatory properties and can improve the skin's elasticity. Exposure to sunlight is how our body generates vitamin D, but since this can be difficult during the autumn and winter months a supplement is recommended during these months. Food sources are unlikely to provide sufficient quantities.
Food sources include: salmon, eggs, soya milk and fortified breakfast cereals and milks.

Vitamin E
Vitamin E is a powerful antioxidant that can protect from harmful UV damage. It is an essential nutrient, so we must obtain it

through our diet and it has anti-inflammatory properties. Vitamin E can be absorbed better when combined with vitamin C.

Food sources include: sunflower seeds, hazelnuts, salmon, spinach, broccoli, wheat germ.

B vitamins

The benefits of B vitamins for skin health range from combating hyperpigmentation and fighting breakouts to softening skin and reducing the appearance of fine lines and wrinkles. Symptoms of vitamin B deficiency include heightened sun sensitivity, skin rashes, cracked lips, acne and dry and flaking skin. When included in the diet B vitamins support energy levels, brain function and cell metabolism. In relation to skin health they have many and varied benefits as outlined below.

In skincare, vitamin B3 (niacinamide) and vitamin B5 (pantothenic acid) are routinely incorporated into topical products. B3 and B5 are suitable for all skin types. B3 can be beneficial for sensitive or acne-prone skin and B5 can work well for hydrating normal to dry skin.

There are 8 forms of B vitamins:

B VITAMIN	FUNCTION	FOOD SOURCES
B1 (thiamine)	Can be helpful for irritated, red or acne-prone skin Anti-ageing properties	Beef, pork, eggs, legumes, tuna
B2 (riboflavin)	Can help improve skin tone Balances natural skin oils	Dairy, eggs, kidney beans, salmon, chicken, lean beef and pork
B3 (niacinamide)	Supports the skin's natural defences Helps to protect against environmental stressors Hydrates and brightens	Potatoes, oats, cottage cheese, mushrooms, peanuts, turkey, chicken, tempeh
B5 (pantothenic acid)	Hydration and suppleness Helps to balance the skin and calm the appearance of redness and inflammation	Shiitake mushrooms, sunflower seeds, chicken
B6 (pyridoxine)	Hormonal balance Can be helpful for hormonal acne, redness and inflammation	Chickpeas, bulgur, raisins, salmon
B7 (Biotin)	Forms part of the structure of keratin, a protein found in hair, skin and nails Helps to give skin a naturally revitalised appearance Suitable for dull and ageing skin	Egg yolks, salmon, meat, soy, sunflower seeds, avocado, spinach
B9 (folic acid or folate)	Can be helpful for congestion or acne as it can help to purify the skin	Asparagus, peas, romaine lettuce
B12 (Cobalamin)	Helps to boost radiance of the skin as it plays a role in how the body uses protein. Can also help to improve the appearance of dark spots and uneven skin tone	Liver, beef, lamb, oysters, nutritional yeast As food sources are mainly animal-based products, supplementation is often recommended to vegans

Pesto avocado pasta

 Skin health Heart health Pregnancy and fertility Vegan

Serves 2

Prep: 10 minutes

Cook: 10 minutes

Nutrients per serving

Calories (kcal) **315**

Carbohydrates (g) **37.5**

Protein (g) **8**

Fat (g) **32**

Ingredients

180g wholewheat pasta
12 cherry tomatoes, halved
1 tbsp pumpkin seeds

For the pesto sauce:
1 large ripe avocado, peeled and
　deseeded
3 cloves garlic
juice of ½ lemon
30g fresh basil, chopped
2 tbsp pasta water
2 tbsp pine nuts
salt and pepper

Our skin loves avocados, which are rich in antioxidants, omega-3s and hydrating vitamin E, and loaded with fibre and vitamin A. Pumpkin seeds contain good amounts of vitamin E and zinc. I make a big batch of this pasta and have it in the fridge for work lunches. You can also use the sauce as a dip with fresh vegetables, crackers or on bagels.

1　Cook the pasta according to the instructions on the packet.
2　Meanwhile, make the pesto sauce by putting all the ingredients in a food processor and blitzing until smooth. Season with salt and pepper to taste.
3　Drain the pasta and toss in the pesto sauce. Serve with halved cherry tomatoes and pumpkin seeds. Can be enjoyed hot or cold.

Almond chia crunch parfait

Skin health

Cognitive health

Gut health

Pregnancy and fertility

Vegetarian

Serves 2

Prep: 10 minutes

Nutrients per serving

Calories (kcal) **360**

Carbohydrates (g) **38**

Protein (g) **10**

Fat (g) **16**

Ingredients

handful of chopped almonds
½ tbsp coconut oil
360g plain almond yoghurt
2 tbsp chia seeds
2 tbsp goji berries
2 tbsp smooth almond butter
1 tbsp honey
40g blueberries
fresh mint leaves, chopped, to
    serve (optional)

This recipe uses almond yoghurt and almonds. Almonds are a good source of vitamin E, an antioxidant that can help fight free radicals, reduce inflammation and maintain skin's elasticity. The body stores vitamin E in the epidermis and dermis. In the sebaceous glands, it forms the base of hair follicles, and it is transported to the skin through sebum. Chia seeds are a great plant-based source of omega-3 fatty acids.

1 Preheat the oven to 200°C/180°C fan/gas mark 6. Roast the chopped almonds on a baking sheet with the coconut oil for 6–7 minutes.

2 Combine the rest of the ingredients (apart from the blueberries) in a large bowl. Mix well and divide between two serving glasses. Top with blueberries and the roasted almonds and some chopped fresh mint, if desired.

Salmon super greens omelette

Skin health   Bone health   Cognitive health

Serves 1

Prep: 5 minutes

Cook: 8 minutes

Nutrients per serving

Calories (kcal) **610**

Carbohydrates (g) **12**

Protein (g) **37**

Fat (g) **42**

Ingredients

3 eggs
1 tbsp fresh chives
salt and pepper
2 spring onions, finely chopped
40g baby leaf spinach, chopped
1 tbsp olive oil
½ ripe avocado, chopped
50g smoked salmon, roughly
   chopped
25g pine nuts

This is perfect for breakfast or brunch. It contains important skin-loving nutrients like omega-3, zinc and selenium. Omega-3 helps reduce inflammation in acne and eczema. Our skin loves spinach as it is a great source of vitamins C, E and A.

1 Gently beat the eggs in a bowl and add the chives, salt and pepper. Add the spring onions and spinach and whisk together.
2 Heat the oil in a frying pan over a medium heat and add the egg mixture, tilting the pan so that the mixture completely covers the base, and cook for 2–3 minutes until nearly set.
3 Add the chopped avocado and smoked salmon, fold in half and cook for a further 2 minutes. Scatter the pine nuts over the omelette. Serve warm or allow to cool and pop into a container for lunch on the go.

Roasted balsamic beet and goat's cheese salad with creamy date dressing

Skin health   Bone health   Cognitive health   Gut health   Hormonal health   Vegetarian

Serves 2

Prep: 25 minutes

Cook: 15 minutes

Nutrients per serving

Calories (kcal) **380**

Carbohydrates (g) **18**

Protein (g) **17**

Fat (g) **26**

Ingredients

260g beetroot, peeled and cut into slices
1 tbsp balsamic vinegar
1 tbsp olive oil
150g kale or salad leaves of choice
6 cherry tomatoes, halved
½ cucumber, chopped
100g goat's cheese round, cut into bite-size pieces
50g walnuts, roughly chopped

For the date dressing:
70g pitted dates
60ml reserved soaking water
2 tbsp balsamic vinegar
3 tbsp soy milk

Goat's cheese provides: calcium, protein, vitamins B6 and A, selenium (which helps to protect against UV-induced damage, including wrinkles, and from inflammation and pigmentation) and probiotics, which provide friendly bacteria for our gut, which in turn can benefit skin health. Massaging the kale makes it more palatable by releasing its bitter compounds and breaking down its fibrous texture. You can store this salad in an airtight container for up to 3 days.

1 Preheat the oven to 200°C/180°C fan/gas mark 6. Grease and line a baking tray with baking paper. Toss the beetroot slices with the olive oil and balsamic vinegar. Put the slices on a baking tray and roast in the oven for 15 minutes.

2 To make the dressing, put the dates in a bowl with enough hot water to cover and let them soak for 20 minutes. Drain, saving 60ml of the soaking water. Put all the dressing ingredients in a food processor or blender and blend until smooth. Add more water if you prefer a thinner consistency.

3 Put the kale in a bowl, pour over the dressing and massage the leaves with your hands. Add the roasted beetroot, tomatoes, cucumber, goat's cheese and walnuts.

Walnut-crusted salmon with sundried tomato couscous

Skin health

Cognitive health

Heart health

Pregnancy and fertility

Serves 4

Prep: 15 minutes

Cook: 15 minutes

Nutrients per serving

Calories (kcal) **580**

Carbohydrates (g) **38**

Protein (g) **41**

Fat (g) **25**

Ingredients

1 clove garlic, minced
1 tsp lemon zest
1 tsp lemon juice
1 tsp chopped rosemary, fresh or dried
1 tsp honey
3 tbsp walnuts, blitzed in a food processor
3 tbsp breadcrumbs
1 tsp olive oil
4 salmon fillets
200g couscous
3 tbsp sundried tomato pesto
1 lemon, sliced into wedges
fresh dill, chopped, to serve (optional)

Salmon and walnuts are great sources of omega-3 fatty acids, and this marinade and walnut crust add a lovely flavour and texture. For couscous I usually use the rule of 1:1; if you are cooking 80g couscous, add 80ml boiling water (or vegetable stock) and cover with a plate for 10–12 minutes, then fluff it up with a fork. A versatile dinner that the whole family will love.

1 Preheat the oven to 200°C/180°C fan/gas mark 6 and line a baking tray with parchment paper.
2 Combine the garlic, lemon zest and juice, chopped rosemary and honey in a small bowl. In a separate bowl combine the crushed walnuts, breadcrumbs and oil.
3 Put the salmon fillets on the baking tray and spread the garlic mixture evenly on each fillet. Sprinkle the breadcrumb mixture over the garlic mixture and bake in the oven for 12–15 minutes or until the fish flakes easily with a fork.
4 Put the dry couscous in a heat-proof bowl, pour over 200ml boiling water, put a plate or tea towel over the bowl and allow to sit for 10 minutes. Then fluff it up with a fork, add the tomato pesto and mix well.
5 Serve the salmon fillets on the couscous with lemon wedges on the side and a sprinkling of fresh dill, if desired.

Two-way mushroom risotto

Skin health

Cognitive health

Gut health

Hormonal health

Serves 4

Prep: 10 minutes

Cook: 35 minutes

Nutrients per serving

Calories (kcal) **445**

Carbohydrates (g) **60**

Protein (g) **15**

Fat (g) **16**

Ingredients

1 tbsp olive oil

1 shallot, finely chopped

200g Portobello mushrooms, chopped

200g shiitake mushrooms, chopped

2 garlic cloves, minced

250g arborio rice

125ml white wine

1 tbsp thyme, fresh or dried, chopped if fresh

500ml chicken stock

40g shaved Parmesan, to serve

handful of pea shoots, to serve (optional)

Two types of mushrooms are used in this recipe; shiitake mushrooms have skin-healing properties and are packed full of antioxidants and anti-inflammatory compounds. Portobello mushrooms are a rich source of C and B vitamins as well as selenium, which can help to slow down skin ageing by improving elasticity. As well as a midweek dinner, this can be stored in a lunchbox in the fridge for the next day.

1 Heat a large frying pan over medium heat, add the oil and sauté the shallot for 3–4 minutes. Add both mushrooms and garlic to the pan and continue to sauté until the mushrooms are golden brown (around 7–8 minutes).

2 Add the rice and cook for 1 minute, stirring continuously. Then add the wine and thyme and stir gently. Cook for 2–3 minutes until most of the liquid has been absorbed.

3 Using a ladle, add chicken stock, 100ml at a time, stirring continuously. Keep stirring and adding liquid stock until the rice is al dente (about 15–20 minutes).

4 Serve warm with Parmesan and pea shoots, if desired, or store in an airtight container in the fridge for up to 3 days.

Carrot cake

Skin health

Vegetarian

Serves 12

Prep: 20 minutes

Cook: 35 minutes

Nutrients per serving

Calories (kcal) **250**

Carbohydrates (g) **65**

Protein (g) **6**

Fat (g) **15**

Ingredients

For the sponge:
265g self-raising flour
zest of ½ orange
2 tsp ground cinnamon
1 tsp ground nutmeg
100ml olive oil
100g plain natural yoghurt
300g brown sugar
2 tsp vanilla extract
4 large eggs
270g carrots (3–4), peeled and
    grated, 1 tbsp reserved for
    decoration

For the icing:
220g low-fat cream cheese
200g icing sugar
50g pecans, to decorate

Carrots contain a plant compound known as beta-carotene, an antioxidant that is converted to vitamin A in the body. It can help to repair skin tissue as well as protecting the skin from the sun's UV rays. Carrots provide natural exfoliation by encouraging cell turnover.

1 Preheat the oven to 200°C/180°C fan/gas mark 6. Lightly grease with olive oil and line two 23cm round cake tins.
2 Whisk together the flour, orange zest, cinnamon and nutmeg in a bowl until combined.
3 In a separate bowl, whisk together the oil, yoghurt, sugar and vanilla extract. Then add the eggs one at a time, whisking after each addition.
4 Add the dry ingredients to the wet ingredients, gently stirring until the batter is smooth. Then add the carrots and mix well.
5 Divide the mixture between the two tins and bake in the centre of the oven for 35 minutes or until a skewer inserted into the centre of the cake comes out dry. Allow the cake to cool fully before icing.
6 Put the cream cheese and icing sugar in a small bowl and beat together. Spoon half the icing mixture over one sponge cake, place the second on top and cover with icing. Decorate the top of the cake with pecans and the reserved grated carrot.

Glowing skin smoothie

Skin health

Vegan

Serves 2

Prep: 5 minutes

Nutrients per serving

Calories (kcal) **200**

Carbohydrates (g) **30**

Protein (g) **4**

Fat (g) **7**

Ingredients

300ml coconut water (or more as needed)
1 banana, chopped and frozen
150g chopped pineapple (fresh or frozen)
150g chopped mango (fresh or frozen)
60g spinach leaves
½ avocado, sliced
1 tbsp maple syrup
handful of ice

Coconut water helps moisturise and hydrate the skin, and another hydration hero is avocado, packed with anti-inflammatory omega-3. Mangoes contain carotenoids, which can help keep our skin glowing. Pineapples are a rich source of vitamin C, which is important for the production of collagen – collagen production naturally decreases as we age. Spinach is nutrient-dense, too, and all the ingredients work together to pack a nutrient punch.

1 Place all the ingredients in a food processor or blender and blend on high for at least 3 minutes until smooth.
2 Add more coconut water as needed if you prefer a thinner consistency.

Vegetarian and vegan health

I like to think of myself as a 'flexitarian' as I eat mostly plant-based food, and have done for many years, but I also eat fish at least once or twice weekly and meat once fortnightly. This is what works for me and although I love eating mainly plant-based, consuming a vegetarian or, more so, a vegan diet can make it more difficult to obtain certain nutrients. If you are a vegetarian or a vegan it is really important to understand how to incorporate enough protein, iron, calcium and vitamin B12 into your diet. Below I will highlight various nutrients that you should plan to incorporate into your meals if you follow a vegan or vegetarian diet and the recipes will showcase how to do that.

Iron

Iron is a major component of haemoglobin, a type of protein in red blood cells that carries oxygen from the lungs to all parts of the body. If your body is lacking in iron there won't be enough red blood cells to store and transport oxygen and this can lead to fatigue. Iron deficiency is the most common nutritional deficiency in the world, affecting about half the world's population. It causes fatigue, pale skin and light-headedness, among other symptoms. Women who are pregnant or menstruating are at the highest risk of developing the condition. Monthly blood loss from periods is one of the main causes of iron loss globally. In addition, vegan and vegetarian diets put you at a higher risk of iron deficiency as the richest sources of iron are animal-based products. Iron is also part of myoglobin, a protein that carries and stores oxygen in muscle tissues.

Iron from food comes in two forms: haem and non-haem iron. Haem iron is found only in animal products like meat, poultry and seafood. Non-haem iron is found in plant-based foods like nuts, seeds, leafy greens and whole grains.

The types of iron we store in our body (liver, muscle, spleen and bone marrow) is called ferritin and it is delivered throughout the body by transferrin, a protein in the blood that binds to iron.

If you're thinking about taking an iron supplement it is important to get your iron levels checked by your doctor first. If you have too much iron, you can develop a condition known as haemochromatosis, or iron overload, which if untreated can damage the liver, pancreas, heart and joints. It can present as severe tiredness. It is usually an inherited condition; in fact it is Ireland's most common inherited disease. In order to develop the condition both your parents must carry the defective gene, and one in five Irish people are carriers of the gene.

Iron-deficiency anaemia
As the name implies, iron-deficiency anaemia is caused by insufficient iron. Without enough iron, your body can't produce enough haemoglobin in red blood cells to allow them to carry oxygen. This is why you may feel tired and short of breath.

Symptoms include: fatigue and light-headedness, cold hands and feet, brittle nails, pale skin and inflammation or soreness of your tongue. In children it can present with a poor appetite.

If you suspect you or your child may have iron deficiency anaemia it is important to see a doctor who can carry out blood tests to diagnose the condition. It is not one to self-diagnose or treat yourself!

Risk factors
- **Pregnancy:** In pregnancy the volume of blood in your body increases, therefore so does the amount of iron you need. Your iron stores must serve your own needs as well as providing a source of haemoglobin for the growing foetus.
- **Menstruation:** Monthly blood loss from menstruation is the leading cause of iron loss globally.
- **Infants and children:** Children who are born prematurely or at a low birth weight who may not get enough iron from breast milk or formula are at risk of deficiency. Children also need extra iron during growth spurts.
- **Vegetarians:** Your body regularly gets iron from the food you eat. Iron-rich sources of food include meat and eggs. Vegetable sources such as leafy greens also provide iron, but this form of iron may be less well absorbed by the body.

The role of vitamin C
Vitamin C-rich foods can enhance the body's ability to absorb iron. Drinking citrus juices or eating foods rich in vitamin C (such as bell peppers, broccoli and tomatoes) at the same time as iron-rich foods can help your body to better absorb dietary iron.

Omegas

Omega-3 fatty acids are a group of polyunsaturated fatty acids. Your body cannot produce omega-3 fatty acids so it is important to obtain them from your diet. The three most important types are ALA (alpha-linolenic acid), DHA (docosahexaenoic acid), and EPA (eicosapentaenoic acid). ALA is mainly found in plants, while DHA and EPA occur mostly in animal foods and algae.

- **ALA:** The most common dietary source of omega-3. It is used for energy in the body and it can be converted to the other two forms of omega-3s, DHA and EPA. However, the conversion process is inefficient as only a small percentage is converted to the active forms. Sources include flaxseed, hemp seeds, canola oil, chia seeds, soybeans and walnuts.
- **EPA:** Found mostly in animal products like oily fish (salmon, mackerel and tuna), fish oil and some microalgae. A small part of EPA can be converted into DHA in the body. If you have no fish or meat at all in your diet it may be worth considering an omega supplement.
- **DHA:** The most important omega-3 fatty acid. It is a key structural component of the retina and the brain. Like EPA, the main source is fatty fish and fish oil. Meat, eggs and dairy from grass-fed animals also contain DHA. Vegans are at a higher risk of DHA deficiency and might consider taking a microalgae supplement to ensure they get enough of this omega-3. DHA is particularly important during pregnancy and breastfeeding as DHA plays a role in the health of the baby.

Vitamin B12

Another essential vitamin that can be hard to obtain through a plant-based diet is vitamin B12. For those following a strict vegan diet, it is one that I would recommend supplementing. B12 is needed to form red blood cells and DNA. It plays a role in many aspects of health, such as supporting bone health, energy levels, cognitive function and mood. It binds to the protein in the food we eat and then, once digested, hydrochloric acid and enzymes in the stomach unbind B12 into its free form. B12 is naturally present in foods of animal origin including fish, meat, poultry, eggs and dairy products. Some cereals are fortified with B12 and it is also available in nutritional yeast, which you can buy in most supermarkets. I like to sprinkle it over my lunches or dinners or even over popcorn! It has a lovely nutty flavour and is a good way to increase B12 intake.

B12 deficiency

Causes of B12 deficiency include difficulty absorbing B12 from food, lack of intrinsic factor (a type of protein our bodies make) as a result of pernicious anaemia, use of certain medications like metformin (an anti-diabetic drug) and proton pump inhibitors, and dietary deficiency.

Symptoms include numbness and tingling in the hands and feet, fatigue, pale skin, an inflamed and swollen tongue (glossitis), and weight loss.

My favourite plant-based ingredients

Although I have highlighted a few supplements that are worth considering if following a strict vegan diet, the recipes in this book contain many delicious and nutritious ingredients that can fulfil your nutrient needs and satisfy your tastebuds!

Ginger

Ginger is part of the same family as cardamom and turmeric and has been used for centuries in China not only for its flavour but as an important ingredient to aid circulation, reduce nausea and help digestion. It is rich in antioxidants, which help to manage free radicals – compounds that can damage cells in large numbers. It is also a diaphoretic, which means that it encourages perspiration and thus aids fevers associated with recovery from influenza and colds. Gingerol, the main bioactive compound in ginger, has powerful anti-inflammatory effects, and some studies have looked at the beneficial role of ginger for conditions like rheumatoid arthritis and osteoarthritis.

Turmeric

Another powerful antioxidant from the same family is turmeric. It has been used in India for thousands of years both as a spice and as a medicinal herb. Recently, drug companies have been looking into the science around the compounds found in turmeric, most notably curcumin. Curcumin has a strong anti-inflammatory effect but it is poorly absorbed by the body, so many people choose to take it as a supplement for conditions like osteoarthritis and joint pain. It can help to include black pepper when cooking with turmeric as black pepper contains piperine, which enhances the absorption of curcumin. Many supplements use a combination of curcumin and piperine.

Garlic

Garlic is another plant-based food that has been valued as a medicinal plant throughout the ages.

It was used in both world wars as an antiseptic to clean and dress wounds. It is a brilliant source of vitamin B6, known to support a healthy heart and reduce blood pressure. Garlic is a plant in the allium (onion) family. Most of the health benefits are gained from sulphur compounds, which are released when garlic is chopped, crushed or chewed. Garlic is also a rich source of manganese, vitamin C and selenium, the latter two of which support immune function. A 12-week study found that a daily garlic supplement reduced the number of colds by 63 per cent compared to a placebo. Some studies have also shown that garlic can reduce the duration of cold symptoms.

Spinach

Spinach, which belongs to the amaranth family, is well known for its nutritional properties. It is rich in iron and vitamin K to support healthy bones and is a good source of vitamins C and B2 as well as magnesium. Its dark green leaves are rich in carotenoids and chlorophyll, which are known to have anti-inflammatory compounds as well as aiding eyesight. It is also a source of folic acid, or vitamin B9, crucial for pregnant women in the first trimester and pre-pregnancy and essential for normal cellular function and tissue growth. (Note: all women of child-bearing age should take a 400mcg folic acid supplement as we do not get enough from our diets alone.)

Adequate protein intake on a vegan diet

Vegans may be more likely to lack sufficient protein in their diets. However, with enough planning and knowledge it is possible to reach your protein targets with plant-based protein sources.

Plant versus animal protein

Protein is made up of amino acids. There are about 20 amino acids found in nature that our bodies use to build protein. Nine of those are essential amino acids, which means that we must obtain them through diet – our body cannot make them. Our body can, however, make the other 11.

Animal protein contains all nine essential amino acids, so it is considered a 'complete' source of protein. On the other hand, many plant-based sources contain some but not all of the essential amino acids. But it is possible to obtain all nine by combining different plant sources. Chia seeds contain all nine essential amino acids!

Bottom line

It is possible to obtain all the essential amino acids by combining different plant sources of protein, for example:
- **Rice + beans**
- **Pita + hummus**
- **Peanut butter + wholewheat bread.**

Sources of essential amino acid include:
- **Lysine:** Soy, quinoa, pumpkin seeds, pistachio, beans
- **Isoleucine:** Lentils, beans, oats, brown rice
- **Leucine:** Peas, wholegrain rice, seaweed, sesame seeds
- **Methionine:** Hemp, chia and sunflower seeds
- **Phenylalanine:** Avocados, almonds, beans, brown rice
- **Threonine:** Leafy greens, hemp and chia seeds
- **Histidine:** Brown rice, potatoes, lentils, chickpeas
- **Valine:** Peanuts, soy, mushrooms
- **Tryptophan:** Spinach, sweet potatoes, oats, walnuts.

Bean and kale ragu

Vegan

Serves 2

Prep: 5 minutes

Cook: 1 hour 10 minutes

Nutrients per serving

Calories (kcal) **180**

Carbohydrate **30**

Protein (g) **12.5**

Fat (g) **2g**

Ingredients

200g tinned cannellini beans
400ml vegetable stock
1 tbsp olive oil
1 onion, chopped
400g tinned chopped tomatoes
1 tsp ground cumin
1 garlic clove, minced
2 bay leaves
1 tsp oregano
1 tsp basil
130g fresh kale
salt and pepper

A super-simple lunch recipe which is full of flavourful herbs and spices and high in fibre. Also stores well for lunch on the go. If you don't like kale you can swap it with spinach – both are good sources of iron. Serve with toasted sourdough for dipping!

1 Drain, rinse and cook the cannellini beans in the vegetable stock over a medium heat for 4–5 minutes until heated through. Drain the beans, reserving the stock.
2 Heat the olive oil in a pan over medium-high heat. Add the onion and cook, stirring, until the onion becomes translucent.
3 Reduce the heat to medium. Stir in the tomatoes, cumin, garlic, bay leaves and the vegetable stock from the beans. Simmer for about 1 hour.
4 Stir in the cannellini beans and continue simmering until the beans are heated through. Stir in the oregano, basil and kale. Season with salt and pepper and serve.

Tofu scramble with roasted cherry tomatoes

Vegan

Hormonal health

Immune health

Serves 2

Prep: 5 minutes

Cook: 25 minutes

Nutrients per serving

Calories (kcal) **220**

Protein (g) **21**

Carbohydrates (g) **6**

Fat (g) **12**

Ingredients

50g cherry tomatoes
2 tbsp olive oil
300g firm tofu
¼ tsp turmeric
½ tsp garlic powder
½ tsp paprika
1 tbsp tahini
2 tbsp nutritional yeast
120ml oat milk
salt and pepper
Sourdough bread, to serve
fresh chives, chopped, to serve

This is my favourite tofu scramble recipe. It has a rich and creamy texture and tastes surprisingly like real scrambled eggs! It is a perfect wholesome Sunday brunch idea, packed with essential vitamins and high in plant-based protein and vitamin B12. I like to serve it with toasted sourdough. You can also add baby spinach or some chopped kale to the sauce – it will wilt in under a minute.

1 Preheat the oven to 220°C/200°C fan/gas mark 7. Put the tomatoes on a baking tray lightly greased with olive oil and lined with baking paper, drizzle with 1 tbsp olive oil, season with salt and pepper and roast for 20 minutes.
2 Meanwhile, drain the tofu and pat dry with a paper towel. Put it in a bowl and use your fingers to break it into small pieces.
3 Make your sauce by combining the turmeric, garlic powder, paprika, tahini, nutritional yeast and oat milk and whisk for 2–3 minutes.
4 Heat a large pan over a medium-high heat with the rest of the oil. Add the tofu to the pan and fry until golden brown (5–7 minutes).
5 Add the sauce and continue frying for a further 2–3 minutes.
6 Add a pinch of salt and pepper and with the roasted cherry tomatoes and a sprinkling of fresh chives on sourdough.

Vegan pancakes with creamy cacao and hazelnut spread

Vegan

Skin health

Serves 2

Prep: 10 minutes

Cook: 15 minutes

Ingredients

For the pancakes:
400g spelt flour or plain flour
2 tbsp baking powder
4 tbsp brown sugar
250ml plant-based milk (oat, almond, soy or coconut)
200ml water
2 tbsp coconut oil, melted, plus a little extra
handful of blueberries, fresh or frozen

For the spread:
250g hazelnuts
1 tbsp vanilla extract
25g cacao powder
80g maple syrup or agave syrup
2 tbsp coconut oil, melted
toppings of your choice, e.g. berries, toasted nuts, coconut yoghurt, maple syrup, etc.

I use spelt flour in this recipe but you can opt for plain or gluten-free flour. Spelt flour is packed with iron, zinc and magnesium and it is also a good source of fibre. I'm all about the toppings when it comes to pancakes, so I've included my favourite homemade cacao and hazelnut spread recipe, which is high in B vitamins and healthy fats and can be stored in the fridge for up to a month.

1. Whisk together the flour, baking powder and sugar in a large bowl.
2. Pour the milk, water, melted coconut oil and blueberries into the bowl with the dry ingredients and stir with a wooden spoon until combined. Try not to overmix the batter to ensure the pancakes are fluffy!
3. Heat a large frying pan over a medium heat and grease the pan with some coconut oil. Drop 2–3 tbsp batter into the pan and cook for 3–4 minutes, until the edges are set and bubbles begin to form. Flip the pancakes over and cook for a further 2–3 minutes until both sides are golden.
4. To make the hazelnut and cacao spread, preheat the oven to 220°C/200°C fan/gas mark 7 and roast the hazelnuts for 8 minutes. Allow them to cool, then rub them together in a tea towel to remove their skins. Put them in a food processor and blend until they develop a buttery consistency. Add the remaining ingredients and blend again until smooth.
5. Serve with toppings of your choice – I've used coconut yoghurt and mixed berries.

Turmeric roasted cauliflower salad with honey, lemon and tahini dressing

Vegetarian   Cognitive health   Immune health   Skin health

Serves 2

Prep: 10 minutes

Cook: 15 minutes

Nutrients per serving

Calories (kcal) **310**

Carbohydrates (g) **13.5**

Protein (g) **9**

Fat (g) **30**

Ingredients

For the salad:
400g cauliflower florets
1 tbsp olive oil
1 tbsp ground turmeric
1 tsp ground cumin
200g baby spinach, washed
½ red onion, halved and thinly
    sliced
6 dates, chopped
40g flaked almonds, toasted

For the dressing:
2 tbsp tahini
1 tbsp lemon juice
1 tbsp honey
1 garlic clove, minced
2 tbsp water

A moreish lunch option which is quick and easy to make. Cauliflower is packed with fibre and B vitamins and tastes delicious roasted in these spices. The dates add a subtle sweetness to the dish. Sprinkle with nutritional yeast for an added B12 boost.

1 Preheat the oven to 200°C/180°C fan/gas mark 6. Coat the cauliflower in the olive oil, turmeric and cumin and roast for 10–15 minutes.

2 Meanwhile, make the dressing. Whisk all the ingredients together, adding the water bit by bit until you have the desired consistency. It should coat the back of a spoon.

3 Put the cauliflower, spinach, onion, dates and half the almonds in a large bowl and toss in the dressing.

4 Garnish with the rest of the almonds to serve.

Vegan beetroot casserole

Vegan

Cognitive health

Heart health

Gut health

Serves 6

Prep: 10 minutes

Cook: 1 hour 30 minutes

Nutrients per serving

Calories (kcal) **180**

Carbohydrate **20**

Protein (g) **6**

Fat (g) 3g

Ingredients

6 small beetroot (about 400g), peeled and halved

1 red onion, sliced into wedges

2 carrots, peeled and cut into chunks

1 small sweet potato, cut into chunks

1 tbsp olive oil

salt and pepper

80g red lentils

1 tbsp tomato purée

1 tbsp red wine vinegar

1 tbsp soy sauce

400ml vegetable stock

2 bay leaves

1 tsp dried thyme

mashed potato or crusty bread, to serve

chopped fresh coriander, to serve (optional)

Beetroot is an excellent source of fibre, folate (vitamin B9), iron and vitamin C. Vitamin C helps the body absorb iron and it is a source of inorganic nitrates, which may reduce the risk of heart disease by lowering blood pressure and increasing nitric oxide formation. Nitric oxide causes the blood vessels to relax and dilate. The lentils supply plant-based protein, fibre, folate and iron.

1 Preheat the oven to 220°C/200°C fan/gas mark 7. Place the beetroot, onion, carrots and sweet potato in a large casserole dish, drizzle with the olive oil and season with a pinch of salt and pepper.

2 Roast in the oven for 30–35 minutes, mixing after 15 minutes. Remove the dish from the oven when the vegetables are starting to crisp. Set aside.

3 Meanwhile, wash and drain the lentils and put them in a large saucepan over medium heat. Add the tomato puree, vinegar, soy sauce, vegetable stock, bay leaves and thyme and bring to the boil. Add the lentil mixture to the casserole dish and put back in the oven for 60 minutes or until the lentils are cooked and the vegetables are soft. Serve over mashed potato or crusty bread with a scattering of fresh coriander, if desired.

Lentil, spinach and coconut dhal

Vegetarian

Gut health

Pregnancy and fertility

Skin health

Serves 6

Prep: 10 minutes

Cook: 35 minutes

Nutrients per serving

Calories (kcal) **355**

Carbohydrate **53**

Protein (g) **12**

Fat (g) **12g**

Ingredients

20g coconut oil

1 onion, finely chopped

25g fresh root ginger, peeled and thinly sliced

3 garlic cloves, finely chopped

2 tsp turmeric

2 tsp cumin

1 tsp chilli powder

200g split lentils, soaked for 30 minutes

400g tinned chopped tomatoes

400g tinned coconut milk

70g raisins

100g fresh spinach leaves

salt and pepper

fat-free plain yoghurt, to serve

pomegranate seeds, flaked almonds and fresh coriander, to serve (optional)

Serving up a whopping 12 plant-based foods, this lentil dhal contains good amounts of fibre, B vitamins, iron and polyphenols. Soaking lentils for roughly 30 minutes before cooking enhances the body's rate of mineral absorption and activates the enzyme phytase, which helps to break down phytic acid (which can cause gas and bloating), lectins and amylase, which makes complex starch easier to digest.

1 Heat the coconut oil in a large pan over a medium heat, add the onions and sauté for 7 minutes. Add the ginger and garlic and sauté for a further 3 minutes.

2 Add the spices, lentils, tomatoes, coconut milk and raisins and simmer over a medium heat for 20 minutes.

3 Add the spinach and cook for a further 5 minutes.

4 Season with salt and pepper and serve with yoghurt. Sprinkle with pomegranate seeds, flaked almonds and fresh coriander, if desired. Also goes well with poppadoms and garlic naan bread.

Vegan lemon no-cheesecake

Vegan

Gut health

Fitness

Pregnancy and fertility

Serves 6

Prep: 10 minutes, plus 1 hour soaking, 2 hours and 30 minutes chilling

Nutrients per serving

Calories (kcal) **300**

Carbohydrates (g) **16**

Protein (g) **7**

Fat (g) **22g**

Ingredients

For the base:
30g coconut oil
100g roasted almonds
100g soft pitted dates

For the filling:
280g cashew nuts
1 tsp vanilla extract
3 tbsp agave syrup
40g coconut oil
150ml coconut milk
2 lemons, zested and juiced

Cheesecake is always a crowd pleaser, but it can be hard to make for vegans. The cashews in this recipe provide a creamy alternative to cheese and supply fibre, protein and magnesium. A guilt-free, delicious dessert option.

1 Put the cashews in a large bowl, add boiling water to cover and set aside for an hour.

2 Meanwhile, blitz all the ingredients for the base in a food processor or blender and pat down tightly into a baking tin lined with baking paper. Put in the fridge for 30 minutes to set.

3 Drain the cashew nuts and add them to a blender along with all the remaining filling ingredients, reserving some lemon zest for serving, and blitz until smooth.

4 Spoon the filling over the base and leave to chill in the fridge for a minimum of 2 hours. Scatter over the reserved lemon zest before serving.

Sweet and salty caramel bars

Vegan

Makes 8 bars

Prep: 15 minutes, plus 1 hour chilling

Nutrients per serving

Calories (kcal) **180**

Carbohydrates (g) **25**

Protein (g) **3.5**

Fat (g) **8**

Ingredients

For the nougat layer:
180g Medjool dates, pitted
100g gluten-free oats, blitzed into
   a fine powder
½ tsp vanilla extract

For the vegan caramel:
70g smooth peanut butter
80g maple syrup
50g salted peanuts, plus extra for
   decoration

For the chocolate topping:
20g cacao powder
50g coconut oil
80g maple syrup

These naturally sweetened dairy- and gluten-free bars are the perfect afternoon snack. It's a no-bake recipe using healthy ingredients that will satisfy any sweet tooth. To make the dairy-free chocolate topping I melt together three ingredients, but you could just melt your favourite vegan chocolate. Store in the fridge if you like a soft caramel or in the freezer if you prefer a chewier texture.

1 Line a 23 x 13cm baking tin with baking paper.
2 To make the nougat layer, pulse the dates, oats and vanilla extract in a food processor. Place this mixture in the bottom of the tin and press down firmly to pack it evenly into the bottom of the tin.
3 To make the caramel, put the peanut butter and maple syrup in a small bowl and stir until combined. Pour the caramel over the nougat layer and use a spatula or spoon to spread evenly. Sprinkle the peanuts over the caramel layer.
4 To make the chocolate topping, put all the ingredients in a saucepan and stir over a low heat for 5 minutes until combined. Pour over the peanuts and use a spatula to distribute evenly. Sprinkle the reserved peanuts on top of the chocolate layer.
5 Put the baking tin in the fridge or freezer for at least 1 hour to set before slicing into 8 bars.

Acknowledgements

I want to start by thanking my husband, Rob. From being my guinea pig and testing all of my weird and wonderful creations, to cleaning up all of my kitchen messes, to providing feedback and support through the whole process – you are my biggest supporter and for that I am eternally grateful.

A special thank you to the incredible team at Gill. Teresa, I would not be writing this without your guidance and support, so thank you for all of the encouragement. To Kristen and Aoibheann, thank you for all of the incredible work you have done to bring this dream of mine into reality.

To all of the girls at the Collaborations Agency, Jess, Lynn and Donna, thank you for being the best agents and supporting me through the process.

Thank you to all of my friends and family for their unwavering support.

Lastly, I would like to thank you, for picking up this book and dedicating your time to reading it. I really hope you gain some valuable information from it.

References

Fitness

Centers for Disease Control and Prevention (online) 'Benefits of Physical Activity' <https://www.cdc.gov/physicalactivity/basics/pa-health/index.htm - :~:text=Being physically active can improve,activity gain some health benefits>. Accessed 3 February 2023.

Chad, M.K., Arent, S., Schoenfeld, B.J., Stout, J.R., Campbell, B., Willborn, C.D., Taylor, L., Kalman, D., Smith-Ryan, A.E., Kreider, R.B., Willoughby, D., Arciero, P.J., VanDusseldorp, T.A., Ormsbee, M.J., Wildman, R., Greenwood, M., Ziegenfuss, T.N., Aragon, A.A. and Antonio, J. (2017) 'International Society of Sports Nutrition position stand: Nutrient timing', *Journal of the International Society of Sports Nutrition* 14:1.

Coyle, E.F. *et al.* (1986) 'Muscle glycogen utilization during prolonged strenuous exercise when fed carbohydrate', *Journal of Applied Physiology* 61(1): 165–72.

Gleeson, M., Nieman, D.C. and Pedersen, B.K. (2004) 'Exercise, nutrition and immune function', *Journal of Sports Sciences* 22(1): 115–25.

Marquet, L.A., Hausswirth, C., Molle, O., Hawley, J. A., Burke, L.M., Tiollier, E. and Brisswalter, J. (2016) 'Periodization of carbohydrate intake: Short-term effect on performance', *Nutrients* 8(12): 755.

Immune health

Childs, Chandra, R.K. (1997) 'Nutrition and the immune system: An introduction', *American Journal of Clinical Nutrition* 1 August, 66(2): 460S–463S.

Calder, P.C and Miles, E.A. (2019) 'Diet and immune function', *Nutrients* 16 August, 11(8).

Green, W.D. and Beck, M.A. (2017) 'Obesity impairs the adaptive immune response to influenza virus', *Annals of the American Thoracic Society* November (Supplement 5): S406–9.

Hemilä, H. and Louhiala, P. (2013) 'Vitamin C for preventing and treating pneumonia', *Cochrane Database of Systematic Reviews* 2013(8).

Li, X.V., Leonardi, I. and Iliev, I.D. (2019) 'Gut mycobiota in immunity and inflammatory disease', *Immunity* 18 June, 50(6): 1365–79.

Skalny, A.V., Rink, L., Ajsuvakova, O.P., Aschner, M., Gritsenko, V.A., Alekseenko, S.I., Svistunov, A.A., Petrakis, D., Spandidos, D.A., Aaseth, J. *et al.* (2020) 'Zinc and respiratory tract infections: Perspectives for COVID-19' (Review) *International Journal of Molecular Medicine* 46:17–26.

Wessels, I., Maywald, M. and Rink L. (2017) 'Zinc as a gatekeeper of immune function', *Nutrients* December, 9(12): 1286.

Cognitive health

Accinni, T. *et al.* (2022) 'A revision on the effectiveness of omega-3 polyunsaturated fatty acids as monotherapy in the treatment of major depressive disorder', *International Journal of Clinical Practice* 16 November: 3801235.

Alasmari F. (2020) 'Caffeine induces neurobehavioral effects through modulating neurotransmitters', *Saudi Pharmaceutical Journal* 28(4): 445–51.

Cremonini, A.L., Caffa, I., Cea, M., Nencioni, A., Odetti, P. and Monacelli, F. (2019) 'Nutrients in the prevention of Alzheimer's disease', *Oxidative Medicine and Cellular Longevity* 9874159.

Engels, L., Tian, X., Govoni, K., Wynn, M. and Smith, B. (2018) 'The effects of poor maternal nutrition on fetal brain development', *Journal of Animal Sciences* 96: 80-102.

Fiolet, T. *et al.* (2018) 'Consumption of ultra-processed foods and cancer risk: Results from NutriNet-Santé prospective cohort', *British Medical Journal* 13: 360.

Gray, K. M., Watson, N. L., Carpenter, M. J. and Larowe, S.D. (2010) 'N-acetylcysteine (NAC) in young marijuana users: An open-label pilot study', *American Journal on Addictions* 19(2): 187–189.

Jacka, F.N *et al.* (2017) 'A randomised controlled trial of dietary improvement for adults with major depression (the 'SMILES' trial)', *BMC Medicine* 15(23).

Minarini, A. et al. (2017) 'N-acetylcysteine in the treatment of psychiatric disorders: Current status and future prospects', *Expert Opinion on Drug Metabolism and Toxicology* 13(3): 279–92.

Schmaal, L. *et al.* (2012) 'N-acetylcysteine normalizes glutamate levels in cocaine-dependent patients: A randomized crossover magnetic resonance spectroscopy study', *Neuropsychopharmacology* 37: 2143–52.

Willett, W.C., Sacks, F., Trichopoulou, A., Ferro-Luzzi, A., Helsing, E. and Trichopoulos, D. (1995) 'Mediterranean diet pyramid: A cultural model for healthy eating', *American Journal of Clinical Nutrition* 61: S1402–S1406.

Hormonal health

Baltgalvis, K.A., Greising, S.M., Warren, G.L. and Lowe, D.A. (2010) 'Estrogen regulates estrogen receptors and antioxidant gene expression in mouse skeletal muscle' *PLOS One* 5(4):101–64.

Barber, T., Dimitriadis, G., Andreu, A. and Franks, S. (2016) 'Polycystic ovary syndrome: Insight into pathogenesis and a common association with insulin resistance', *Clinical Medicine* 16(3): 262–6.

Centers for Disease Control and Prevention (online) 'Heavy Menstrual Bleeding' <https://www.cdc.gov/ncbddd/blooddisorders/women/menorrhagia.html>. Accessed 15 November 2022.

Franco, O.H. (2016) 'Use of plant-based therapies and menopausal symptoms: A systematic review and meta-analysis' *Journal of the American Medical Association* 21 June 315(23): 2554–63.

Glycemic Index Foundation (online) 'What is Low GI?' <https://www.gisymbol.com/low-gi-explained>.

Glycemic Index Foundation (online) 'GI Science and Latest Emerging Research' <https://www.gisymbol.com/gi-science-and-latest-emerging-research>.

International Diabetes Federation (2021) *Diabetes Atlas*. Available at https://diabetesatlas.org. Accessed 10 November 2022.

Jakubowicz, D. *et al.* (2013) 'Effects of caloric intake timing on insulin resistance and hyperandrogenism in lean women with polycystic ovary syndrome', *Clinical Science* May.

Messina, M., Duncan, A., Messina, V., Lynch, H., Kiel, J. and Erdman, J.W. Jr (2022) 'The health effects of soy: A reference guide for health professionals', *Frontiers in Nutrition* 11 August 9:970364. <doi: 10.3389/fnut.2022.970364> eCollection 2022.

Morley, L., Tang, T., Yasmin, E., Norman, R. and Balen, A. (2017) 'Insulin-sensitising drugs (metformin, rosiglitazone, pioglitazone, D-chiro-inositol) for women with polycystic ovary syndrome, oligo amenorrhoea and subfertility' (review), *Cochrane Database of Systematic Reviews* Issue 11.

Parazzini, F., Di Martino, M. and Pellegrino, P. (2017) 'Magnesium in the gynecological practice: A literature review', *Magnesium Research* 30(1): 1–7 <https://doi.org/10.1684/mrh.2017.0419>.

Rietjens, I.M.C.M., Louisse, J. and Beekmann, K. (2017) 'The potential health effects of dietary phytoestrogens', *British Journal of Pharmacology* June 174(11): 1263–80.

Rodríguez-García, C., Sánchez-Quesada, C., Toledo, E., Delgado-Rodríguez, M. and Gaforio, J.J. (2019) 'Naturally lignan-rich foods: A dietary tool for health promotion?', *Molecules* 6 March 24(5): 917.

Shukla, A., Iliescu, R., Thomas, C. and Aronne, L. (2015) 'Food order has a significant impact on postprandial glucose and insulin levels', *Diabetes Care* 38(7):e98–e99 <doi:10.2337/dc15-0429>.

Willett, W. and Liu, S. (2019) 'Carbohydrate quality and health: Distilling simple truths from complexity', *American Journal of Clinical Nutrition* 110(4):803–4 <doi:10.1093/ajcn/nqz215>.

Gut health

McDonald, D., Birmingham, A. and Knight, R. (2015) 'Context and the human microbiome', *Microbiome* 3, 52.

McDonald, D, *et al.* (2018) 'American Gut: an Open Platform for Citizen Science Microbiome Research', *mSystems*, 3 (3).

Huttenhower, C., Gevers, D., Knight, R., Abubucker, S., Badger, J.H., Chinwalla A.T., *et al.* (2012) 'Structure, function and diversity of the healthy human microbiome', *Nature* 486:207–14.

Heart health

American Heart Association (online) 'Managing Blood Pressure with a Heart-Healthy Diet' <https://www.heart.org/en/health-topics/high-blood-pressure/changes-you-can-make-to-manage-high-blood-pressure/managing-blood-pressure-with-a-heart-healthy-diet>. Accessed 2 March 2023.

Chiavaroli, L. *et al.* (2019) 'DASH dietary pattern and cardiometabolic outcomes: An umbrella review of systematic reviews and meta-analyses', *Nutrients* 11(2).

Estruch, R., Ros, E., Salas-Salvadó, J. *et al.* (2018) 'Study Investigators. Primary prevention of cardiovascular disease with a Mediterranean diet supplemented with extra-virgin olive oil or nuts', *New England Journal of Medicine* 378: e34.

Irish Hospice Foundation and Trinity College Dublin (2021) *Dying and Death in Ireland: What do We Routinely Measure, How can We Improve?* <http://Dying-and-Death-in-Ireland-what-do-we-routinely-measure-how-can-we-improve-2021.pdf>. Accessed 1 March 2023.

Martínez-González, I., Gea, A. and Ruiz-Canela, M. (2019) 'The Mediterranean diet and cardiovascular health', *Circulation Research* 124: 779–98.

O'Keeffe, M. (2023) 'Gaps in cardiovascular care contributing to deaths of over 9,000 people per year', Irish Heart Foundation 28 February 2023 <https://irishheart.ie/news/gaps-in-cardiovascular-care-contributing-to-deaths-of-over-9000-people-per-year/>. Accessed 2 March 2023.

Tapsell, L.C., Neale, E.P., Satija, A. and Hu, F.B. (2016) 'Foods, nutrients, and dietary patterns: Interconnections and implications for dietary guidelines', *Advanced Nutrition* 7: 445–54.

Bone health

Health Service Executive (online) 'Vitamin D' <https://www2.hse.ie/conditions/vitamins-and-minerals/vitamin-d/>. Accessed on 28 February 2023.

Heaney, R.P. and Layman, D.K. (2008) 'Amount and type of protein influences bone health', *American Journal of Clinical Nutrition* 87(5).

Lorincz, C., Manske, S.L. and Zernicke, R. (2009) 'Bone health. Part 1: Nutrition', *Sports Health* 1(3): 253–60.

NIH National Institute of Arthritis and Musculoskeletal and Skin Diseases (online) 'Osteoporosis Overview' <https://www.bones.nih.gov/health-info/bone/osteoporosis/overview - :-:text=Osteoporosis is a bone disease,of fractures (broken bones)>. Accessed 22 February 2023.

Vannucci, L., Fossi, C., Quattrini, S., Guasti, L., Pampaloni, B., Gronchi, G., Giusti, F., Romagnoli, C., Cianferotti, L., Marcucci, G. and Brandi, M. L. (2018) 'Calcium intake in bone health: A focus on calcium-rich mineral waters', *Nutrients* 10(12).

Pregnancy and fertility

Alahmar, A.T. (2019) 'The impact of two doses of coenzyme Q10 on semen parameters and antioxidant status in men with idiopathic oligoasthenoteratozoospermia', *Clinical and Experimental Reproductive Medicine* 46(3) <doi: 10.5653/cerm.2019.00136>.

American College of Obstetricians and Gyndecologists (ACOG) (2010) 'Moderate Caffeine Consumption during Pregnancy' < https://www.acog.org/clinical/clinical-guidance/committee-opinion/articles/2010/08/moderate-caffeine-consumption-during-pregnancy?utm_source=redirect&utm_medium=web&utm_campaign=otn>.

Ben-Meir, A. *et al.* (2015) 'Coenzyme Q10 restores oocyte mitochondrial function and fertility during reproductive aging', *Aging Cell* 14(5): 887–95 <doi: 10.1111/acel.12368>.

Eskew, A., Bligard, K., Broughton D.E. *et al.* (2017) 'Does alcohol intake impact ovarian reserve?', *Fertility and Sterility* 108(3): E258.

Hanson *et al.* (2015) 'The International Federation of Gynecology and Obstetrics (FIGO) recommendations on adolescent, preconception, and maternal nutrition: "Think Nutrition First"', *International Journal of Gynecology and Obstetrics* 131(S4): S213–S252 <https://obgyn.onlinelibrary.wiley.com/doi/epdf/10.1016/S0020-7292%2815%2930034-5>.

HSE (online) 'Healthy Eating During Pregnancy' < https://www2.hse.ie/pregnancy-birth/keeping-well/food-drink/healthy-eating>.

Izadi, A., Ebrahimi, S., Shirazi, S., Taghizadeh, S., Parizad, M., Farzadi, L. and Gargari, B.P. (2019) 'Hormonal and metabolic effects of coenzyme Q10 and/or vitamin E in patients with polycystic ovary syndrome', *Journal of Clinical Endocrinology and Medicine* 104(2): 319–27.

Precision Nutrition (online) 'What to Eat During Pregnancy' <https://www.precisionnutrition.com/what-to-eat-during-pregnancy-infographic>

Precision Nutrition, 'All about Healthy Fats' <https://www.precisionnutrition.com/all-about-healthy-fats>.

Xu, Y., Nisenblat, V., Lu, C., Li, R., Qiao, J., Zhen, X. and Wang, S. (2018) 'Pretreatment with coenzyme Q10 improves ovarian response and embryo quality in low-prognosis young women with decreased ovarian reserve: A randomized controlled trial', *Reproductive Biology and Endocrinology* 16(1): 29 <doi: 10.1186/s12958-018-0343-0>.

Skin health

Black, H.S. and Rhodes, L.E. (2016) 'Potential benefits of omega-3 fatty acids in non-melanoma skin cancer', *Journal of Clinical Medicine* 4 February, 5(2):23.

De Mel, D. and Suphioglu, C. (2014) 'Fishy business: Effect of omega-3 fatty acids on zinc transporters and free zinc availability in human neuronal cells', *Nutrients* 6(8): 3245–58.

Pilkington, S.M., Watson, R.E.B., Nicolaou, A. and Rhodes, L.E. (2011), 'Omega-3 polyunsaturated fatty acids: photoprotective macronutrients', *Experimental Dermatology* 20: 537-543.

Sikora, M., Stec, A., Chrabaszcz, M., Knot, A., Waskiel-Burnat, A., Rakowska, A., Olszewska, M. and Rudnicka, L. (2020) 'Gut microbiome in psoriasis: An updated review', *Pathogens* 9: 463.

Szántó, M., Dózsa, A., Antal, D., Szabó, K., Kemény, L. and Bai, P. (2019) 'Targeting the gut–skin axis—Probiotics as new tools for skin disorder management?' *Experimental Dermatology* 28: 1210–18.

Wei, D., Zhang, L., Williams, D.L. and Browder, I.W. (2002) 'Glucan stimulates human dermal fibroblast collagen biosynthesis through a nuclear factor-1 dependent mechanism', *Wound Repair and Regeneration* 10: 161–8 <https://doi.org/10.1046/j.1524-475X.2002.10804.x>.

Vegetarian/vegan health

Barceló-Coblijn, G. and Murphy, E.J. (2009) 'Alpha-linolenic acid and its conversion to longer-chain n-3 fatty acids: benefits for human health and a role in maintaining tissue n-3 fatty acid levels', *Progress in Lipid Research* 48(6): 355–74 doi: 10.1016/j.plipres.2009.07.002.

Deckelbaum, R.J. and Torrejon C. (2012) 'The omega-3 fatty acid nutritional landscape: Health benefits and sources; *Journal of Nutrition* March, 142(3): 587S-591S doi: 10.3945/jn.111.148080.

Langan, R.C. and Goodbred, A.J. (2017) 'Vitamin B12 deficiency: Recognition and management'. *American Family Physician* 96: 384–9.

Nannicini, F., Sofi, F., Avanzi, G., Abbate, R. and Gensini G.F. (2006) 'Alpha-linolenic acid and cardiovascular diseases omega-3 fatty acids beyond eicosapentaenoic acid and docosahexaenoic acid', *Minerva Cardioangiology* August, 54(4):431-42. PMID: 17016414.

Stabler, S.P. (2020) 'Vitamin B12' in B.P. Marriott, D.F. Birt, V.A. Stallings and A.A. Yates (eds), *Present Knowledge in Nutrition*, 11th edn, pp. 257–71. Washington, DC: Elsevier.

Tallaght University Hospital (online) 'Hereditary Haemochromatosis' <https://www.tuh.ie/Departments/Gastroenterology/Hereditary-Haemochromatosis.html - :-:text=Hereditary Haemochromatosis is Ireland's most,potential to develop iron overload>.

Index

A

adaptogens 87

ageing 32

alcohol 125, 129, 172, 193

almond butter
    Almond butter and date oat pots 133
    Almond chia crunch parfait 199
    Apple pie overnight oats 109
    Five-minute no-bake protein bars 27
    Superfood smoothie bowl 157

almond milk
    Anti-nausea smoothie 191
    Apple pie overnight oats 109
    Brain-boosting chocolate delights 73
    Greek yoghurt chocolate mousse 120
    Superfood smoothie bowl 157

almonds 85, 109
    Almond chia crunch parfait 199
    Lamb tagine 46
    Seed cycling granola 89
    Turmeric roasted cauliflower salad with honey, lemon & tahini dressing 222
    Vegan lemon no-cheesecake 229

Alzheimer's disease 56, 57, 58

amaretto, Cherry Basque cheesecake with cherry coulis 167

amino acids 6–7, 35, 55–6, 216
    sources 28, 87, 143, 156, 194

anaemia 213–14, 215

Anti-nausea smoothie 191

Antioxidant-rich root vegetable soup 93

antioxidants 56, 57, 87, 126, 135
    coenzyme Q10 (CoQ10) 171
    sources 163, 182, 194, 206, 215

apples 79, 102, 103
    Apple and blackberry oat crumble 145
    Apple pie overnight oats 109
    Waldorf salad with prawns 72

arthritis 31, 157, 167, 215

asparagus, Cheddar, onion and asparagus frittata 40

aubergines
    Baba ghanoush 75
    Hummus-crusted chicken with zesty lemon quinoa 20
    Turkey moussaka 187

autoimmune conditions 31, 32, 33

avocados 102
    Balanced bagel 13
    Brain-boosting chocolate delights 73
    Butternut breakfast bowl 63
    Fish tacos with tomato salsa 139
    Glowing skin smoothie 211
    Goat's cheese and avocado smash 15
    Mexican scramble 107
    Miso salmon and sweet potato 119
    Pesto avocado pasta 197
    Salmon super greens omelette 200
    Tofu Buddha bowl with coconut peanut sauce 135
    Turkey burgers with butternut boats 97

B

Baba ghanoush 75

bacteria
    beneficial 35, 111, 118, 202
    dysbiosis 195
    gut bacteria 33, 54, 104, 105, 111, 118, 202
    prebiotics and 37, 109
    probiotics and 105

Baked sweet potato chilli 16

Balanced bagel 13

bananas 79, 102
    Anti-nausea smoothie 191
    Glowing skin smoothie 211
    Oat bran raspberry muffins 111
    Post-workout chocolate coconut overnight oats 11
    Strawberry and banana baked oats 179
    Superfood smoothie bowl 157

beans 85
    Bean and kale ragu 217
    see also black beans; cannellini beans; green beans; kidney beans

beef
    Baked sweet potato chilli 16
    Comforting sweet potato cottage pie 23

beetroot 225
    Antioxidant-rich root vegetable soup 93
    Roasted balsamic beet and goat's cheese salad with creamy date dressing 202
    Vegan beetroot casserole 225

Benecol spread
    Apple and blackberry oat crumble 145
    Cottage pie 183
berries 56, 57, 85, 194
    Apple and blackberry oat crumble 145
    see also blueberries; goji berries; raspberries;
        strawberries
beta-carotene 56
beta-glucan 194
black beans
    Lime and black bean prawns with brown rice 161
    Mexican scramble 107
    Tofu Buddha bowl with coconut peanut sauce 135
blueberries 57, 102, 194
    Almond chia crunch parfait 199
    Post-workout chocolate coconut overnight oats 11
    Roasted fig fruit bowl 155
    Vegan pancakes with creamy cacao and hazelnut
        spread 221
bone health 148–52
    bone cells 149
    calcium, role of 150–2
    gender 150
    lifestyle factors 149–50
    osteoporosis 149, 150
    vitamin D 85, 150, 151, 152
Brain-boosting chocolate delights 73
bread/breadcrumbs 79
    Fakeaway KFC burger 141
    French toast 177
    Mexican scramble 107
    Oaty breakfast bread 61
    Quinoa veggie burger with roasted red pepper relish 19
    Salmon fishcakes 65
    Tofu scramble with roasted cherry tomatoes 219
    Walnut-crusted salmon with sundried tomato
        couscous 205
broccoli 56, 85
    Antioxidant-rich root vegetable soup 93
    Halloumi and broccoli salad 41
bulgur wheat, Greek-style cod with bulgur wheat 71
butternut squash
    Butternut breakfast bowl 63
    Red pepper and butternut pasta 47
    Thai-style butternut tofu curry 165
    Turkey burgers with butternut boats 97

C

cacao powder
    Chocolate protein pudding 28
    Maca chia pudding 87
    No-bake dark chocolate cashew bars 98
    Sweet and salty caramel bars 231
    Vegan pancakes with creamy cacao and hazelnut
        spread 221
caffeine 56, 57, 175
calcium
    birth–9 years 151
    bone health and 150–2
    early adulthood: 20–30 years 151
    middle adulthood: 30–50 years 151–2
    over-50s and menopausal women 152
    over-70s 152
    pregnancy 150, 175
    puberty: 10–20 years 151
    sources 85, 87, 150–1, 155, 161, 168, 202
cannellini beans
    Bean and kale ragu 217
    One-pot chicken and leek traybake 69
    Quinoa veggie burger with roasted red pepper relish 19
Caramelised banana porridge 37
carbohydrates 7–8, 59, 79–80, 173
carotenoids 33, 211, 216
carrots 79
    Antioxidant-rich root vegetable soup 93
    Carrot cake 209
    Carrot and miso soup 118
    Chicken bone broth 159
    Chicken noodle soup 39
    Comforting sweet potato cottage pie 23
    Cottage pie 183
    Lentil Bolognese 115
    Nourishing veggie bowl 182
    Tahini mango salad 66
    Vegan beetroot casserole 225
cashew nuts
    Brain-boosting chocolate delights 73
    Carrot and miso soup 118

Healthy honey fruit tart 49

No-bake dark chocolate cashew bars 98

Tahini mango salad 66

Vegan lemon no-cheesecake 229

cauliflower 85, 104, 222

Gut-loving chickpea and cauliflower salad 113

Nourishing veggie bowl 182

Turmeric roasted cauliflower salad with honey, lemon
and tahini dressing 222

celery

Chicken bone broth 159

Chicken noodle soup 39

Comforting sweet potato cottage pie 23

Cottage pie 183

Lentil Bolognese 115

Waldorf salad with prawns 72

Cheddar cheese

Cheddar, onion and asparagus frittata 40

Cottage pie 183

Fish pie 94

Spicy stuffed peppers 42

Sweet potato and cheese frittata 181

Turkey flatbread 180

cheese

Comforting sweet potato cottage pie 23

see also Cheddar cheese; cottage cheese; cream cheese;
feta; goat's cheese; mozzarella; Parmesan;
ricotta

Cherry Basque cheesecake with cherry coulis 167

cherry supplements 167

cherry tomatoes

Butternut breakfast bowl 63

Cherry tomato egg-white muffins 131

Fish tacos with tomato salsa 139

Gut-loving chickpea and cauliflower salad 113

Halloumi and broccoli salad 41

Pesto avocado pasta 197

Roasted balsamic beet and goat's cheese salad with
creamy date dressing 202

Spinach and pesto pasta 137

Tofu scramble with roasted cherry tomatoes 219

chia seeds 85, 194, 216

Almond chia crunch parfait 199

Anti-nausea smoothie 191

Apple pie overnight oats 109

Maca chia pudding 87

chicken

Chicken bone broth 159

Chicken noodle soup 39

Cottage pie 183

Creamy chicken stroganoff 21

Fakeaway KFC burger 141

Hummus-crusted chicken with zesty lemon quinoa 20

Mexican chicken salad 162

One-pot chicken and leek traybake 69

Tomato chicken pasta bake 163

chickpea fusilli, Spinach and ricotta fusilli 24

chickpeas 79

Coconut chickpea curry 117

Creamy tahini hummus 51

Falafel salad with tahini dressing 91

Gut-loving chickpea and cauliflower salad 113

Lamb tagine 46

Nourishing veggie bowl 182

chocolate 56, 57, 85

Brain-boosting chocolate delights 73

caffeine content 175

Chocolate protein pudding 28

Five-minute no-bake protein bars 27

flavonoids 56, 57

Greek yoghurt chocolate mousse 120

No-bake dark chocolate cashew bars 98

Seed cycling granola 89

White and dark chocolate mousse 189

cholesterol 8, 9, 124, 125–8, 133

choline 127, 181

cinnamon 85

coconut/coconut milk 102

Coconut chickpea curry 117

Lentil, spinach and coconut dhal 227

Post-workout chocolate coconut overnight oats 11

Seed cycling granola 89

Steamed yellow fish curry 185

Thai-style butternut tofu curry 165

Tofu Buddha bowl with coconut peanut sauce 135

Vegan lemon no-cheesecake 229

cod

Fish tacos with tomato salsa 139

Greek-style cod with bulgur wheat 71

Steamed yellow fish curry 185

cognitive behavioural therapy (CBT) 83, 102

cognitive decline 57–8

cognitive health 52–9
  gut-brain connection 54
  nutrition 55–8
  pregnancy 56–7
  processed foods 54–5
  recommended diets 57–8
  SMILES trial 53
collagen 168, 194, 195, 211
Comforting sweet potato cottage pie 23
cottage cheese
  Baked sweet potato chilli 16
  Fish tacos with tomato salsa 139
  Miso salmon and sweet potato 119
  Turkey burgers with butternut boats 97
  Turkey flatbread 180
Cottage pie 183
courgettes
  Coconut chickpea curry 117
  Hoisin duck noodles 143
  Turkey burgers with butternut boats 97
couscous
  Gut-loving chickpea and cauliflower salad 113
  Nourishing veggie bowl 182
  Walnut-crusted salmon with sundried tomato couscous 205
cream cheese
  Balanced bagel 13
  Carrot cake 209
  Cherry Basque cheesecake with cherry coulis 167
  White and dark chocolate mousse 189
Creamy chicken stroganoff 21
Creamy tahini hummus 51
cucumbers 102
  Falafel salad with tahini dressing 91
  Hoisin duck noodles 143
  Hummus-crusted chicken with zesty lemon quinoa 20
  Mexican chicken salad 162
  Roasted balsamic beet and goat's cheese salad with creamy date dressing 202
  Tofu Buddha bowl with coconut peanut sauce 135
cysteine (amino acid) 55–6

D
dates 102
  Almond butter and date oat pots 133
  Brain-boosting chocolate delights 73
  Falafel salad with tahini dressing 91
  Healthy honey fruit tart 49
  No-bake dark chocolate cashew bars 98
  Roasted balsamic beet and goat's cheese salad with creamy date dressing 202
  Sweet and salty caramel bars 231
  Turmeric roasted cauliflower salad with honey, lemon and tahini dressing 222
  Vegan lemon no-cheesecake 229
diabetes 32, 78–9, 173
diet
  balanced diet 33
  cognitive health and 57–8
  DASH (dietary approach to stop hypertension) 58, 126
  heart-healthy nutrition 127
  higher-protein/low-carbohydrate plan 85
  hormones, impact on 82
  immunity and 32
  Mediterranean diet 57, 125–6
  Mediterranean-DASH diet intervention for neurodegenerative delay (MIND) 58
  personalised approach 58–9
  vegan/vegetarian diet 213–16
dried fruit
  Lamb tagine 46
  Lentil, spinach and coconut dhal 227
duck, Hoisin duck noodles 143

E
egg whites 128
  Cherry tomato egg-white muffins 131
  Chocolate protein pudding 28
  French toast 177
eggs 55, 127–8
  Balanced bagel 13
  Butternut breakfast bowl 63
  Carrot cake 209
  Cherry Basque cheesecake with cherry coulis 167
  Fakeaway KFC burger 141
  Falafel salad with tahini dressing 91
  Mexican scramble 107
  Oaty breakfast bread 61
  Quinoa veggie burger with roasted red pepper relish 19
  Salmon super greens omelette 200
  Strawberry and banana baked oats 179
  Sweet potato and cheese frittata 181

Turkey burgers with butternut boats 97

enzymes 105, 227

exercise 9–10, 82–3, 85, 129

F

Fakeaway KFC burger 141

Falafel salad with tahini dressing 91

fats 8–9

    healthy fats 193–4

    monounsaturated fats 8, 126

    polyunsaturated fats (PUFAs) 8–9, 57, 126

    pregnancy: recommended daily intake 174

    saturated (bad) fats 9, 128

    sources 175

    unsaturated (good) fats 8

fermented foods 101

feta

    Butternut breakfast bowl 63

    Hummus-crusted chicken with zesty lemon quinoa 20

    Tahini mango salad 66

fibre 87, 103, 104–5

    hormone balance and 82

    pregnancy: daily intake 173–4

    sources 109, 113, 174, 183, 222, 225, 229

figs 102

    Roasted fig fruit bowl 155

fish 55, 56, 85, 175

    Fish pie 94

    Fish tacos with tomato salsa 139

    see also cod; haddock; prawns; salmon; sea bass; tuna

Five-minute no-bake protein bars 27

flavonoids 56, 57, 105

folate/folic acid 56, 171, 225

French toast 177

fruit 102, 103, 104

    Healthy honey fruit tart 49

G

gamma-linolenic acid (GLA) 77–8

garlic, medicinal value of 215–16

ginger (fresh) 215

Glowing skin smoothie 211

glycaemic index (GI) 79–80

goat's cheese

    Goat's cheese and avocado smash 15

Roasted balsamic beet and goat's cheese salad with creamy date dressing 202

goji berries

    Almond butter and date oat pots 133

    Almond chia crunch parfait 199

grains and starches 102, 103, 104

grapes 85, 102, 194

    Waldorf salad with prawns 72

Greek yoghurt

    Almond butter and date oat pots 133

    Creamy chicken stroganoff 21

    Greek yoghurt chocolate mousse 120

    Healthy honey fruit tart 49

    Post-workout chocolate coconut overnight oats 11

    Roasted fig fruit bowl 155

    Superfood smoothie bowl 157

    Waldorf salad with prawns 72

Greek-style cod with bulgur wheat 71

green beans 104

    Steamed yellow fish curry 185

gut health 85, 100–5

    CNS (central nervous system) 101

    CNS-ENS connection 102

    digestive issues 101

    emotional symptoms 101

    ENS (enteric nervous system) 101–3

    fermented foods 101

    fibre, facts on 104–5

    gut-brain axis 102

    gut-skin axis 195

    IBS (irritable bowel syndrome) 101–3

    IBS–C (IBS with constipation) 101

    neurotransmitters 103

    supplements 105

    thirty plants a week 103–4

gut-friendly glossary 105

Gut-loving chickpea and cauliflower salad 113

H

haddock

    Fish pie 94

    Fish tacos with tomato salsa 139

haemochromatosis 125, 213

Halloumi and broccoli salad 41

hazelnuts

    Caramelised banana porridge 37

Halloumi and broccoli salad 41
Vegan pancakes with creamy cacao and hazelnut
    spread 221
Healthy honey fruit tart 49
heart health 122–9
    arrythmia 125
    atherosclerosis 124
    cardiomyopahty 124–5, 129
    cardiovascular disease (CVD) 32, 55, 123–5
    cholesterol 124, 125–8
    congestive heart failure 124
    coronary artery disease (CAD) 124
    DASH diet 126
    eggs 127–8
    exercise 129
    foods to avoid 128–9
    heart valve disease 124
    heart-healthy nutrition 127
    saturated fats 128
    sodium intake 128
    sugars 128
herbs (fresh) 102
Hoisin duck noodles 143
honey
    Almond chia crunch parfait 199
    Antioxidant-rich root vegetable soup 93
    Caramelised banana porridge 37
    Halloumi and broccoli salad 41
    Healthy honey fruit tart 49
    Lamb tagine 46
    Miso salmon and sweet potato 119
    Quinoa veggie burger with roasted red pepper
        relish 19
    Roasted fig fruit bowl 155
    Seed cycling granola 89
    Sizzling ginger sea bass 45
    Superfood smoothie bowl 157
    Tahini mango salad 66
    Turmeric roasted cauliflower salad with honey, lemon
        and tahini dressing 222
    Waldorf salad with prawns 72
hormonal health 76–86
    cortisol 32, 86
    diabetes 78–9
    diet, impact of 82, 85
    endocrine system 78–80, 86

female hormones 80
follicle-stimulating hormone (FSH) 81, 82
glycaemic index (GI) 79–80
hyperthyroidism 78
hypothyroidism 78
insulin 78–9, 84
insulin resistance 79–80, 82, 84
insulin sensitivity 84–5
insulin-like growth factor 1 (IGF-1) 194
luteinising hormone (LH) 81, 82
macronutrient balance 82
menopause 80, 85
menstrual cycle 80, 81–3
metabolism and 78
oestrogen 77, 80, 82–3
PCOS (polycystic ovary syndrome) 32, 77, 79, 82, 84–5
PMDD (premenstrual dysphoric disorder) 83
PMS/PMS treatment options 83–4, 86
progesterone 77, 81
seed cycling 77–8
SSRIs 83
thyroid hormones 78
hummus
    Creamy tahini hummus 51
    Hummus-crusted chicken with zesty lemon quinoa 20
hydration 9–10, 59, 84, 193

I

immune system
    acquired/adaptive immunity 31
    boosting 33–5
    factors affecting 31–2
    innate immune system 31
inflammation 31–2, 84, 200
    chronic 32, 54, 86, 195
inulin 105, 113
iron 32, 35
    absorption 35, 214, 225
    deficiency 35, 213–14
    ferritin 213
    haem iron 213
    haemochromatosis 213
    menstruation, loss during 80, 213
    non-haem iron 213
    pregnancy and 174
    sources 35, 87, 182, 213, 221, 225, 227

supplements 58–9, 80, 213
    vegetarians/vegans 213
    vitamin C and 35, 182, 214, 225
iron-deficiency anaemia 213–14
irritable bowel syndrome (IBS) 101–3

K

kale 56, 85
    Bean and kale ragu 217
    Butternut breakfast bowl 63
    Kale chips 168
    Roasted balsamic beet and goat's cheese salad with
        creamy date dressing 202
kidney beans 85
    Baked sweet potato chilli 16
    Mexican chicken salad 162
kiwis, Roasted fig fruit bowl 155

L

Lamb tagine 46
leeks, One-pot chicken and leek traybake 69
legumes 55, 85, 102, 104
lentils 85
    Lentil Bolognese 115
    Lentil, spinach and coconut dhal 227
    Vegan beetroot casserole 225
lettuce
    Falafel salad with tahini dressing 91
    Fish tacos with tomato salsa 139
    Mexican chicken salad 162
    Salmon and salsa pitta pockets 153
    Waldorf salad with prawns 72
Lime and black bean prawns with brown rice 161
lutein 56
lycopene 163, 194

M

maca powder
    Maca chia pudding 87
    Superfood smoothie bowl 157
macronutrients 5
magnesium 82, 155, 221, 229
mangoes
    Anti-nausea smoothie 191
    Glowing skin smoothie 211
    Tahini mango salad 66

    Tofu Buddha bowl with coconut peanut sauce 135
mayonnaise
    Fakeaway KFC burger 141
    Salmon and salsa pitta pockets 153
    Tuna and sweetcorn baked potato 140
meat 55, 194
menstrual cycle 80, 81–2
    exercise 82–3
    follicular phase 81–2
    iron-deficiency anaemia 80, 214
    luteal phase 82
    menstrual phase 81
    ovulatory phase 82
    PMS 83–4
    premenstrual dysphoric disorder (PMDD) 83
metabolic disorders 125
Mexican chicken salad 162
Mexican scramble 107
microbiome 35, 195
micronutrients 5, 33
minerals 126
    see also iron; magnesium; zinc
miso
    Butternut breakfast bowl 63
    Carrot and miso soup 118
    Miso salmon and sweet potato 119
    Tofu Buddha bowl with coconut peanut sauce 135
mozzarella
    Spicy stuffed peppers 42
    Tomato chicken pasta bake 163
    Turkey moussaka 187
mushrooms 194
    Creamy chicken stroganoff 21
    Two-way mushroom risotto 206

N

neurological disorders 56
neurotransmitters 59, 103
nitric oxide 225
No-bake dark chocolate cashew bars 98
noodles
    Chicken bone broth 159
    Chicken noodle soup 39
    Creamy chicken stroganoff 21
    Hoisin duck noodles 143
Nourishing veggie bowl 182

nutrition, brain function and 55–7
nutritional psychiatry 53
nuts 55, 85, 102, 104
    see also cashews; hazelnuts; peanuts; pecans; pine nuts;
        pistachios; walnuts

O

oat milk
    Maca chia pudding 87
    No-bake dark chocolate cashew bars 98
    Tofu scramble with roasted cherry tomatoes 219
oats/oat bran 79
    Almond butter and date oat pots 133
    Apple pie overnight oats 109
    Caramelised banana porridge 37
    Five-minute no-bake protein bars 27
    Maca chia pudding 87
    No-bake dark chocolate cashew bars 98
    Oat bran raspberry muffins 111
    Oaty breakfast bread 61
    Post-workout chocolate coconut overnight oats 11
    Seed cycling granola 89
    Strawberry and banana baked oats 179
    Sweet and salty caramel bars 231
Oaty breakfast bread 61
obesity 32, 35, 55, 79, 125, 129
omega-3 56–7, 59, 193–4
    ALA 56, 214
    anti-inflammatory properties 193
    DHA 56–7, 94, 214
    EPA 56, 94, 214
    mood disorders and 57
    plant-based sources 199
    PMS symptoms and 84
    pre-natal depression and 174
    pregnancy and 174
    skin conditions and 174, 193, 200
    sources 56, 85, 87, 109, 194, 205, 211, 214
    types of 56
    vegetarian sources 194
omega-6 174, 193
One-pot chicken and leek traybake 69
osteoarthritis 167, 215
osteoporosis 85, 149, 150, 152, 157

P

Parkinson's disease 56
Parmesan
    Lentil Bolognese 115
    Spinach and ricotta fusilli 24
    Tomato chicken pasta bake 163
    Turkey moussaka 187
    Two-way mushroom risotto 206
Parmesan-free pesto 147
pasta 79
    Lentil Bolognese 115
    Pesto avocado pasta 197
    Red pepper and butternut pasta 47
    Spinach and pesto pasta 137
    Spinach and ricotta fusilli 24
    Tomato chicken pasta bake 163
peanuts/peanut butter
    Anti-nausea smoothie 191
    No-bake dark chocolate cashew bars 98
    Post-workout chocolate coconut overnight oats 11
    Sweet and salty caramel bars 231
    Tofu Buddha bowl with coconut peanut sauce 135
peas 79
    Fish pie 94
    Goat's cheese and avocado smash 15
pecans
    Carrot cake 209
    Lentil Bolognese 115
peppers
    Coconut chickpea curry 117
    Hummus-crusted chicken with zesty lemon quinoa 20
    Mexican chicken salad 162
    Mexican scramble 107
    Quinoa veggie burger with roasted red pepper relish 19
    Red pepper and butternut pasta 47
    Spicy stuffed peppers 42
    Tuna and sweetcorn baked potato 140
    Turkey burgers with butternut boats 97
    Turkey flatbread 180
pesto
    Cherry tomato egg-white muffins 131
    Parmesan-free pesto 147
    Pesto avocado pasta 197
    Spinach and pesto pasta 137
phosphorus, sources 87, 161
pine nuts 85

Parmesan-free pesto 147
Pesto avocado pasta 197
Salmon super greens omelette 200
pineapples
Glowing skin smoothie 211
Salmon and salsa pitta pockets 153
pistachios 85
Roasted fig fruit bowl 155
polycystic ovary syndrome (PCOS) 32, 77, 79, 82, 84
polyphenols 105, 107, 120, 227
Post-workout chocolate coconut overnight oats 11
potatoes 79
Cottage pie 183
Fish pie 94
One-pot chicken and leek traybake 69
Tuna and sweetcorn baked potato 140
prawns
Lime and black bean prawns with brown rice 161
Waldorf salad with prawns 72
prebiotics 35, 37, 105, 109, 113, 115, 195
pregnancy and fertility 170–5
additional calories 173–5
alcohol 172
anaemia 214
caffeine consumption 175
calcium 150, 175
carbohydrates 173
coenzyme Q10 (CoQ10) 171
DHA (docosahexaenoic acid) 214
fats 174
fibre 173
folic acid 171
foods to avoid 173, 175
gestational diabetes 173
intrauterine growth restriction (IUGR) 175
iron 174
omegas 174
pre-natal depression 174
protein 173
stress 172
trying to conceive (TTC) 171–2
premenstrual syndrome (PMS) 82–4
probiotics 35, 103, 105, 155, 195, 202
processed foods 54–5, 82
protein 6–7, 35, 59
amino acids 35, 216

hormone production and 82
plant versus animal protein 216
plant-based 182, 216, 219, 225
pregnancy 173
sources 87, 173, 194, 229
vegan diet and 216
protein powder 7
Five-minute no-bake protein bars 27
Post-workout chocolate coconut overnight oats 11

Q
quinoa
Butternut breakfast bowl 63
Hummus-crusted chicken with zesty lemon quinoa 20
Mexican chicken salad 162
Quinoa veggie burger with roasted red pepper relish 19
Tahini mango salad 66
Tofu Buddha bowl with coconut peanut sauce 135

R
raspberries 103, 194
Oat bran raspberry muffins 111
Post-workout chocolate coconut overnight oats 11
recipe icons 4
Red pepper and butternut pasta 47
rice 79
Coconut chickpea curry 117
Lime and black bean prawns with brown rice 161
Two-way mushroom risotto 206
ricotta, Spinach and ricotta fusilli 24
Roasted balsamic beet and goat's cheese salad with creamy date dressing 202
Roasted fig fruit bowl 155

S
salmon 57
Fish pie 94
Miso salmon and sweet potato 119
Salmon fishcakes 65
Salmon and salsa pitta pockets 153
Salmon super greens omelette 200
Walnut-crusted salmon with sundried tomato couscous 205
salt (sodium) 128
schizophrenia 56

sea bass
    Sizzling ginger sea bass 45
Seed cycling granola 89
seeds 55, 77, 102, 104, 194
    Goat's cheese and avocado smash 15
    Gut-loving chickpea and cauliflower salad 113
    Hoisin duck noodles 143
    Nourishing veggie bowl 182
    Pesto avocado pasta 197
    Seed cycling granola 89
    Tahini mango salad 66
    see also flaxseeds; pumpkin seeds; sunflower seeds
selenium 2–6, 32, 34, 46, 159, 202
Sizzling ginger sea bass 45
skin conditions
    acne 193, 195, 196, 200
    eczema 174, 193, 195, 200
    omega-3 and 174, 193, 200
    psoriasis/rosacea 195
skin health 192–6
    antioxidant-rich fruit 194
    beta-glucan 194
    collagen 168, 194, 211
    food tips 193–4
    gut-skin axis 195
    healthy fats 193–4
    hydration 193
    inflammatory skin conditions 195
    prebiotics and 195
    probiotics and 195
    protein and 194
    vitamins 195–6
sleep 32, 33, 84
SMILES 53
sour cream, Cherry Basque cheesecake with cherry
    coulis 167
Spicy stuffed peppers 42
spinach 56, 57, 85, 216
    Anti-nausea smoothie 191
    Coconut chickpea curry 117
    Falafel salad with tahini dressing 91
    Glowing skin smoothie 211
    Gut-loving chickpea and cauliflower salad 113
    Lentil, spinach and coconut dhal 227
    Miso salmon and sweet potato 119
    Nourishing veggie bowl 182

One-pot chicken and leek traybake 69
Salmon super greens omelette 200
Spinach and pesto pasta 137
Spinach and ricotta fusilli 24
Sweet potato and cheese frittata 181
Thai-style butternut tofu curry 165
Tomato chicken pasta bake 163
Turkey burgers with butternut boats 97
Turmeric roasted cauliflower salad with honey, lemon
    and tahini dressing 222
Steamed yellow fish curry 185
strawberries 103, 194
    Greek yoghurt chocolate mousse 120
    Strawberry and banana baked oats 179
stress 32, 54, 84, 86, 101, 172, 195
sugar/sugars 59, 82, 84, 86, 128
sundried tomatoes
    Fakeaway KFC burger 141
    Walnut-crusted salmon with sundried tomato
        couscous 205
Superfood smoothie bowl 157
sweet potatoes
    Baked sweet potato chilli 16
    Comforting sweet potato cottage pie 23
    Gut-loving chickpea and cauliflower salad 113
    Miso salmon and sweet potato 119
    Salmon fishcakes 65
    Sweet potato and cheese frittata 181
    Vegan beetroot casserole 225
Sweet and salty caramel bars 231
sweetcorn
    Chicken noodle soup 39
    Mexican chicken salad 162
    Tofu Buddha bowl with coconut peanut sauce 135
    Tuna and sweetcorn baked potato 140

T

tahini
    Baba ghanoush 75
    Butternut breakfast bowl 63
    Creamy tahini hummus 51
    Falafel salad with tahini dressing 91
    Tahini mango salad 66
    Tofu scramble with roasted cherry tomatoes 219
    Turmeric roasted cauliflower salad with honey, lemon
        and tahini dressing 222

Thai-style butternut tofu curry 165
tofu
    Tahini mango salad 66
    Thai-style butternut tofu curry 165
    Tofu Buddha bowl with coconut peanut sauce 135
    Tofu scramble with roasted cherry tomatoes 219
tomatoes 163, 194
    Baked sweet potato chilli 16
    Bean and kale ragu 217
    Comforting sweet potato cottage pie 23
    Greek-style cod with bulgur wheat 71
    Lamb tagine 46
    Lentil, spinach and coconut dhal 227
    Red pepper and butternut pasta 47
    Spicy stuffed peppers 42
    Tomato chicken pasta bake 163
    Turkey flatbread 180
    Turkey moussaka 187
    see also cherry tomatoes; sundried tomatoes
Tuna and sweetcorn baked potato 140
turkey
    Balanced bagel 13
    Spicy stuffed peppers 42
    Turkey burgers with butternut boats 97
    Turkey flatbread 180
    Turkey moussaka 187
turmeric 85, 215
Turmeric roasted cauliflower salad with honey, lemon
    and tahini dressing 222
turnips, Antioxidant-rich root vegetable soup 93
Two-way mushroom risotto 206

V

Vegan beetroot casserole 225
Vegan lemon no-cheesecake 229
Vegan pancakes with creamy cacao and hazelnut
    spread 221
vegans *see* vegetarian and vegan health
vegetables 55, 56, 58, 102, 103, 104
vegetarian and vegan health 212–16
    amino acids, sources of 216
    anaemia, iron-deficiency 213–14
    DHA deficiency 214
    iron 35, 213–14
    omega-3 sources 194
    omegas and 214

    plant-based ingredients 215–16
    protein 216
    vitamin B12 215
    zinc 34
vitamin A 32, 33, 159, 200, 202
vitamin B1 (thiamine) 75, 87, 196
vitamin B2 (riboflavin) 33, 87
vitamin B3 (niacinamide) 196
vitamin B5 (pantothenic acid) 196
vitamin B6 (pyridoxine) 75, 196, 202
vitamin B7 (Biotin) 196
vitamin B9 (folate) 196, 225
vitamin B12 (Cobalamin) 46, 54, 180, 213, 215
    sources 87, 147, 180, 196, 215, 219
vitamin C 32, 33–4
    collagen and 168, 195, 211
    iron absorption and 35, 182, 214, 225
    sources 33, 87, 195, 200, 206, 211, 225
vitamin D 32, 34, 83, 195
    bone health and 85, 150, 151, 152
    deficiency 34, 82
    sources 34, 195
vitamin D$_2$ 34
vitamin D$_3$ 34
vitamin E 32, 77
    skin health and 195–6, 199
    sources 77, 196, 199, 200
vitamin K 56, 118, 159, 168
vitamins 8, 34
    B vitamins 83, 118, 196, 206, 221, 227

W

Waldorf salad with prawns 72
walnuts 85, 194
    Brain-boosting chocolate delights 73
    Lentil Bolognese 115
    nutritional value 56, 57
    Roasted balsamic beet and goat's cheese salad with
        creamy date dressing 202
    Waldorf salad with prawns 72
    Walnut-crusted salmon with sundried tomato
        couscous 205
weight loss 5, 85
White and dark chocolate mousse 189

wine
    Lentil Bolognese 115
    One-pot chicken and leek traybake 69
    Two-way mushroom risotto 206

Y

yeast (nutritional)
    Kale chips 168
    Parmesan-free pesto 147
    Tofu scramble with roasted cherry tomatoes 219
yoghurt
    Almond chia crunch parfait 199
    Carrot cake 209
    Gut-loving chickpea and cauliflower salad 113
    Lentil, spinach and coconut dhal 227
    Oat bran raspberry muffins 111
    Oaty breakfast bread 61
    Tuna and sweetcorn baked potato 140
    see also Greek yoghurt

Z

zinc 32, 34, 77, 82
    sources 34, 46, 87, 159, 161, 200, 221